'Islam Issa is one of the st
equable, original and sage, t
to with startling, exhilaratin

> Ewan Fernie, *Fellow and Chair, The Shakespeare Institute*

'I have long been a serious fan of Islam Issa and his fresh, open and unflinching perspective on Shakespeare. The illuminating clarity he brings to Shakespeare's resonance and difficulty across cultures and histories is making an essential contribution to twenty-first-century Shakespeareans.'

> Erica Whyman OBE, *Deputy Artistic Director,*
> *Royal Shakespeare Company*

'Islam Issa has a profound understanding of the relationship between culture and our intellectual, social, and political values. His groundbreaking work has important significance for the development of international understanding and for the furtherance of humane values.'

> Sir Stanley Wells, *Honorary President,*
> *Shakespeare Birthplace Trust*

Shakespeare

and Terrorism

Shakespeare and Terrorism delves into how extremists have responded to Shakespeare – whether they've attacked him or been inspired by him – and investigates what the playwright and his works can tell us about the nature, psychology, and consequences of terror.

Literary critic and historian Islam Issa takes readers on a journey from Shakespeare's Stratford-upon-Avon and London to a variety of locations: from Western Europe to the Balkans to the US, from North Africa to the Persian Gulf to Central Asia, and from the theatre to the digital world. Considering incidents from Shakespeare's time through today, including the Gunpowder Plot and 9/11, as well as pivotal figures from *Hamlet* and *Macbeth* to Hitler and Bin Laden, this book brings to light new ideas about key characters, events, and themes both in Shakespeare's plays and the world around them.

A thrilling and accessible read, this ground-breaking book will enlighten and engage students, researchers, and general readers interested in Shakespeare, social sciences, history, and the complex relationships between life and art.

Islam Issa is Reader in Literature and History at Birmingham City University, UK. He is a multi-award-winning writer, curator, and broadcaster. His books include *Milton in the Arab-Muslim World* and he has presented such documentaries as *Cleopatra and Me: In Search of a Lost Queen*.

Spotlight on Shakespeare
Series Editors: John Garrison and Kyle Pivetti

Spotlight on Shakespeare offers a series of concise, lucid books that explore the vital purchase of the modern world on Shakespeare's work. Authors in the series embrace the notion that emergent theories, contemporary events, and movements can help us shed new light on Shakespeare's work and, in turn, his work can help us better make sense of the contemporary world. The aim of each volume is two-fold: to show how Shakespeare speaks to questions in our world and to illuminate his work by looking at it through new forms of human expression. Spotlight on Shakespeare will adopt fresh scholarly trends as contemporary issues emerge, and it will continually prompt its readers to ask, "What can Shakespeare help us see? What can he help us do?"

Spotlight on Shakespeare invites scholars to write non-exhaustive, pithy studies of very focused topics – with the goal of creating books that engage scholars, students, and general readers alike.

Available in this series:

Shakespeare on the Shades of Racism
Ruben Espinosa

Shakespeare in Jest
Indira Ghose

Shakespeare and Terrorism
Islam Issa

For more information about this series, please visit: www. routledge.com/Spotlight-on-Shakespeare/book-series/ SOSHAX

ISLAM ISSA

Shakespeare
and Terrorism

Routledge
Taylor & Francis Group

LONDON AND NEW YORK

First published 2022
by Routledge
2 Park Square, Milton Park, Abingdon, Oxon OX14 4RN

and by Routledge
605 Third Avenue, New York, NY 10158

Routledge is an imprint of the Taylor & Francis Group, an informa business

British Library Cataloguing-in-Publication Data
A catalogue record for this book is available from the British Library

Library of Congress Cataloging-in-Publication Data
A catalog record has been requested for this book

ISBN: 978-0-367-33482-6 (hbk)
ISBN: 978-0-367-33483-3 (pbk)
ISBN: 978-0-429-32008-8 (ebk)

DOI: 10.4324/9780429320088

Typeset in Joanna MT
by Newgen Publishing UK

For...
Iman El-Sharkawy (Mama)
Omneya Abdelsalam
Angelica Duran
Beverley Sherry
Sarah Wood

Contents

Illustrations

Acknowledgements

When I first thought of exploring Shakespeare and terrorism, I actually had a radio documentary in mind. It materialised as a Sunday Feature on BBC Radio 3, airing in 2018 on the eve of Bonfire Night (or Guy Fawkes Night), the annual occasion on which millions of Brits publicly celebrate the foiling of a terror plot! So it is only right to thank Robyn Read and Matthew Dodd for commissioning a project that might otherwise have vanished. The producer, Sara Jane Hall, was instrumental as I articulated my thought processes around the narrative; another producer, Fiona McLean, has enhanced my understanding of lucidity. For the programme, I interviewed three guests, each of whom made expert contributions when we recorded and as I proceeded with the book: Imran Awan, Paul Edmondson (who continues to add value to my life), and Ewan Fernie (who continues to demonstrate allyship).

I had not envisioned writing a book about the topic until John Garrison and Kyle Pivetti bought me an espresso in a Chicago hotel bar just a couple of hours after I had landed. I like to think that it wasn't the jet lag that swayed me to sign up for the idea, but the clear and exciting vision that they had for this series. Working with them has since proven to be a pleasure, as has been the case with the editor, Polly Dodson, whose enthusiasm sealed the deal. The proposal was read by four anonymous reviewers who offered useful comments. For reading and commenting on a full draft, I thank my dear friend David Currell. For valuable conversations and insights, my thanks to Ahmed Al-Dawoody, Soudabeh Ananisarab, Peter Cameron, Matthew Geary, Helen Hopkins, Tony Howe, Mahmood Karimi-Hakak, Rawan Sharaf Khatib, Thomas Knowles, Gemma Moss, Mario Murgia, David Roberts, and Erin Sullivan. For valuable support, Yvette Burn, Andrew Kehoe, and Rosalyn Sklar. And for helping me see the vistas between the cracks, B.L. A couple of anecdotes expand on my *Shakespeare in South Asia* exhibition at the Shakespeare Birthplace Trust (2017), for which my students Gemma Miller and Noor Mear provided research assistance. Much travel has helped inform aspects of this book, including trips to Algeria, Palestine, and Denmark, funded respectively by the British Council, Erasmus+, and Birmingham City University. The university's School of English granted me a research sabbatical and its Faculty of Arts, Design and Media covered the costs of the figures and index, compiled by Nick de Somogyi. Rebecca Rideal kindly allowed me to use her painting for the front cover. Much of this book was penned during a stay as Visiting Scholar at San Diego State University. I am grateful to colleagues there and particularly to Peter Herman for facilitating the visit and for his unfailing support, not least in the form of cheerful chats over food and drink – and alongside Meryl Maneker, for being so welcoming. I must have written about half of the book from Genteel Coffee in downtown San Diego. In California, I was blessed to make two lifelong friends in Damon Dong and Katsiaryna Pashkevich. My parents have been an immovable and moving source of love. My globe-trotting cat Mimi has remained the most loyal writing companion. And Alaa has been the love of my life: I have "not skill enough your worth to sing" but am immensely thankful for your insightful, inspiring, and incredible company.

I dedicate this book to five wonderful women spanning five different continents, each of whose support has been invaluable to my development.

Edinburgh 2021

Introduction: Terror

Identity, freedom, symbolism

He smiled (and smiled) at his daughter. She tried to keep up with every word he was saying but it wasn't easy, given how speedily he was mumbling and how worn out the cheap blue biro pen had become. He stroked three fingers through his long, grey beard as he recollected the memories from all those decades ago. Memories that had stuck with him. Though these were his very first visits to Europe, the images were rapidly becoming more vivid as he spoke. "I generated an impression that, basically, they are loose people", he reflected. From the corner of his eye, he proudly glimpsed his son nodding in agreement. "Though my age didn't allow me to form a complete picture of living there". He was only thirteen back then; he was now in his mid-fifties.

It was the summer of 1970. London's big department stores were full of hustling shoppers. Oxford's cobbled streets made for anxious bike rides. His step-dad had sent him to England but he was still wondering whether it was his self-made, billionaire father, the owner of a construction empire, who had actually funded this trip for his seventeenth son (an only-child of his mum but with no fewer than twenty-three half-brothers and thirty-three half-sisters). Either way, he was there to learn English – and to see the world. He had also been sick lately and his family preferred for him to get treatment in Europe. Now, his silence emphasised the repetitive sound

DOI: 10.4324/9780429320088-1

of the spinning ceiling fan. His daughter looked up from the page in anticipation. He was remembering the weekends from that summer in England, especially those weekly day-trips he was forced to go on. One trip, in particular, had to be mentioned.

"And we went every Sunday to Shakespeare's house", he recalled, his daughter scribbling.

He pressed his lips together, shaking his head subtly: "But I did not like that, and I saw that they were a society different from us, and that theirs was a morally loose society".

Osama Bin Laden was assassinated just months later, shortly after midnight on 2 May 2011 in Abbottabad, Pakistan. The CIA discovered a cache of documents and files in his hide-away, some to which they already had access and others that were new. They were made public in late 2017. The terrorist mastermind of the world-changing 9/11 attacks on the US had been watching Mr. Bean, Shaun the Sheep, and Wallace and Gromit. He had saved around 200 YouTube clips, including a version of the viral "Charlie bit my finger". He also had a sizeable library and a substantial stash of pornography. One of the new, revelatory items was a beige notebook. The words "private diary" are centred on its first page, followed by 220 packed pages in handwritten, blue, sometimes red, biro. The CIA scanned and read every page of this journal almost imme-diately. Its entries continue until the day before his death. While I may have added my own imagined details to his writing process, the Arabic entry is, in translation, exactly as quoted already:

> I generated an impression that, basically, they are loose
> people. Though my age didn't allow me to form a complete

picture of living there. And we went every Sunday to Shakespeare's house. But I did not like that, and I saw that they were a society different from us, and that theirs was a morally loose society.

And there is much else that is likely to be true: that this entry was written in his hideaway compound and that one or more of his other children and perhaps his wife were also present. Most often, the diary takes the form of a recorded conversation, a question and answer session between father (Bin Laden) and son (Khalid, in his early twenties). Both were killed in the raid. At times, the conversation extends to the entire family: one of his wives, another son of similar age (Hamza, who would go on to marry the daughter of the lead 9/11 hijacker and become a leading figure in al-Qaeda until he was killed in mid-2019), and two daughters (Miriam and Somaya, in their early twenties and late teens respectively). Rather like the memorable Henry Fuseli and Mihály Munkácsy paintings (1794 and 1877) of the blind John Milton dictating *Paradise Lost*, one of Bin Laden's daughters is thought to have put the pen to paper as he dictated. But it isn't clear whether the dialogue is real or whether Bin Laden is actually indulging in a monologue, asking himself the questions before answering them. The written conversations are so smooth and civil that the latter isn't unlikely.

It would be a little irresponsible to treat the personal journal of one of history's most famous terrorists as a merely personal piece of writing. Of course, first and foremost, its personal side is important. This is clear in the fact that it has an epigraph on the opening page, consisting of lines of poetry about piety, which was probably the first thing to go in the book. As a personal work, it proves that the trip to Shakespeare's birthplace was an unforgettable memory for Bin Laden, and in the context of the conversation, a formative one. But it is also true that the journal's format, regardless of whether the family was present, adds an educating element to the material. If his children were present, he is teaching them; if they weren't, then one can imagine them being invited to read it. Perhaps his children serve as symbols, too, for his followers worldwide, ready to learn from their leader's experiences and reflections. Finally, as someone who became famous during his own lifetime, acutely aware of his own status (as though it needs proving, items recovered from his compound included the documentaries *Biography: Osama Bin Laden* and *Where in the World Is Osama Bin Laden?*), he probably knew that his journal would be read, maybe even analysed, well after his death. His vexation with Shakespeare, then, represents more than just a personal grudge.

Similarly, one cannot assume that it is Shakespeare's birthplace itself that so irritated Bin Laden. Hundreds of thousands of teenagers visit the immaculately preserved half-timbered Tudor house and its garden. I have seen them peer with vastly differing levels of wonderment into the wooden cradle where one the most loved Brits of all time once lay as a mewling and puking baby. Some seem to love it, are inspired by it. And some, presumably, get bored and go home disgruntled, muttering about dead poets. So why did this teenager dislike it so much? And why, when he became one of the most notorious people on the planet, did he remain bothered by Shakespeare, Stratford-upon-Avon embedded into his memories of those formative years? While the most obvious conclusion would appear to be that, in Bin Laden's mind, a dislike of the West and one of its all-time canonical icons simply became conflated, there is much more to this entry. At this important juncture in the journal – the description of his first ever experience of the West – he recalls Shakespeare's birthplace as evidence for his unmoving and devastatingly influential convictions about the West's "morally loose society", in turn differentiating it from his own utopian vision of society. Indeed, much of the journal describes his own ideas of a better world: one which, by all means, is full of apocalyptic moments, not least when he reminisces a dream in which he is personally confronting US tanks. One of the most recurring words throughout is "revolution". What will result, he suggests, is the unity of "the Islamic countries", a unity so strong that peace with the West will one day prevail. Even that could be read apocalyptically: in Islamic eschatology, one sign of the end times is prevailing peace.

Today, the threat of terror looms ominously over Shakespeare's hometown. In 2018, with vehicular hit-and-run terror attacks on the rise in the UK and France, the county council decided that security bollards should be fixed outside Stratford-upon-Avon's Royal Shakespeare Company to limit the threat of attacks on theatregoers. At the Shakespeare birthplace house, to which Bin Laden was referring, bag searches are now standard procedure. Shakespeare's links to terror – or fear of terror – are not theoretical, but have manifestations in everyday reality. In fact, one day, after meetings at the Shakespeare Birthplace Trust, I sat at a café directly across the road. Since it was a rather rare sunny afternoon, I decided to sit outside, just off the pedestrian pavement on a road in which no cars are ordinarily allowed. All in a matter of seconds, a sudden, short police siren made me look up from my laptop. Heavily armed police (any armed police make for an unusual sight in the UK, let alone such firearms as these) jumped out of a barely stationary SUV and sprinted in my direction! Thankfully, they stopped just short of me, staring at a suitcase that had eluded my sight just a few metres in front of where I was sitting. They asked if it was mine – it certainly wasn't and was probably left behind by a big group of tourists some minutes earlier – before the road was shut off and the café evacuated. As I started my premature walk back to the train station, rather baffled that my peaceful cappuccino was interrupted in such dramatic fashion, I contemplated whether something about Shakespeare makes him inevitably susceptible to terror. Does he *have* to be, I wondered, in order to fulfil some sort of national duty?

Nothing is quite so nationalistic as what's under threat of attack, be it concrete (like Westminster) or abstract (like democratic values). While I do not sign up to Samuel Huntington's *Clash of Civilizations* due to its binary generalisations, there is something to be said about the creation and perpetuation of narratives of difference (something Huntington is also guilty of doing). More negatively put, difference can blur into a form of opposition. It's hard to hide from the fact that on the face of it, it's very easy for Shakespeare to represent a vague notion of a British and even Western ideal. This is exemplified, for instance, in random but telling polls about the most loved Brits to have lived, or how the Allies utilised Shakespeare in both World War One and World War Two, or more recently, in his starring role during the opening ceremony of London's 2012 Olympics. Walter Raleigh sums up such a sentiment in his British Academy lecture of July 1918, at a pivotal time of World War One as the Allies were making serious gains:

> I think there is no national poet, of any great nation
> whatsoever, who is so completely representative of his own

people as Shakespeare is representative of the English.
There is certainly no other English poet who comes near to
Shakespeare in embodying our character and our foibles.
No one, in this connexion, would venture even to mention
Spenser or Milton.

He goes on to suggest, presumably with some serious-
ness: "Our critics, at home and abroad, accuse us of arrogance. I doubt if we can prove them wrong; but they do not
always understand the nature of English arrogance".[1] The
plural pronouns – "our", "us", "we" – in themselves position Shakespeare's nation in opposition to the others, to
"them". So, if a national icon is perceived to be under attack,
this serves to cement its iconic status. If this can be achieved
through the accentuation of convincing oppositions, it has
even more strength.

It is not that the threat of violent extremism in Stratford
or elsewhere is not real, but a climate of fear is also a tool of
power and control that has, historically, taken many different
forms. Today, we have cyber threats, health scares, and fear of
immigrants, to name but a few. Shakespeare, too, knew the
importance of fear in social and political contexts. Some of
Shakespeare's characters control plots through such environ-
ments of fear – before they even leap into action. The Roman
general Coriolanus, for instance, is constantly described in
anticipatory dread. From the start, Titus Lartius talks of the
fear Coriolanus inflicts by his mere presence:

with thy grim looks and
The thunder-like percussion of thy sounds
Thou mad'st thine enemies shake

(1.4.59–61)[2]

Introduction

When Coriolanus is rumoured to be returning to Rome after exile, he is feared before he arrives and before the news is even confirmed: "He'll shake your Rome about your ears" (4.6.103). In *Richard III*, much of the protagonist's ability to manoeuvre towards the throne is cemented by his construction of a frightful environment: "I'll make a corpse of him that disobeys" (1.2.37). It is little surprise that various forms of the word "fear" appear hundreds of times in the plays, particularly those concerned with governance and control like *Richard III*, *Julius Caesar*, and *Henry VI, Part Two*.[3] Over the years, critics have assumed that Shakespeare wrote *Macbeth* in his own climate of fear after the biggest terror plot England has ever seen, the Gunpowder Plot, which originated in his hometown. Fear is, moreover, particularly prevalent in the wider reception of Shakespeare. Recently, the Thai filmmaker Ing Kanjanavanit explained the governmental censorship of her *Macbeth* adaptation, *Shakespeare Must Die* (2011), as being a result of the country's "climate of fear". The movie, funded ironically by Thailand's Ministry of Culture, was banned outright due to its allusions to previous coups in the country and references to the Thammasar University Massacre of 1976, when the state attacked thousands of students protesting against the return of exiled former military dictator Thanom Kittikachorn to the country.[4]

From Papists to the plague, from the US to Jews, from the Soviet Union to Islamists, there will always be, to borrow George W. Bush's phrase, some alleged "axis of evil" in existence. As Tony Blair, then British prime minister, announced the "War on Terror" in 2001, he declared: "This is a battle with only one outcome: our victory, not theirs". The question of identity is at play here, but today and with some hindsight, it is even less clear who "we" are, who "they" are, and what "victory" should look like. In 2002, Blair's government released the investigative *September Dossier* (full name: *Iraq's Weapons of Mass Destruction: The Assessment of the British Government*) which ultimately led to the invasion of Iraq in 2003. It included a foreword by the prime minister specifying that Iraq's "military planning allows for some of the WMD to be ready within 45 minutes of an order to use them",[5] leading to the memorable headline in the top-selling UK newspaper: "BRITS 45mins FROM DOOM". Writing about the US government's repeated use of the phrase "War on Terror", Zbigniew Brzezinski, the country's former National Security Advisor, notes:

> the vagueness of the phrase was deliberately (or instinctively) calculated ... Constant reference to a "war on terror" did accomplish one major objective: it stimulated the emergence of a culture of fear. Fear obscures reason, intensifies emotions and makes it easier for demagogic politicians to mobilize the public on behalf of the policies they want to pursue.[6]

Of course, this is nothing new. The Nazis, for instance, used simple, un-nuanced fear tactics expertly to garner support, as stated by Hermann Göring, the war criminal Hitler appointed as minister without portfolio, who said during the Nuremberg Trials that it was "easy" to bring people on your side: "All you have to do is tell them they are being attacked".

So it all fits into place that Shakespeare – both concrete (like his birthplace) and abstract (like his embodiment of "British values") – should be declaredly in danger. We "misunderestimate" the threat at our own peril!

Returning to Bin Laden's journal entry, then, we may need to ask some different questions. By writing about this as an adult, could this actually be a skewed or manipulated perception of the past? Did he really go to the birthplace "every Sunday" or is this hyperbole about having to go more than once? In fact, "Shakespeare's house" could refer to the different family homes in Stratford or, more strikingly, be a euphemism for the theatre, so he could see Shakespeare. More importantly, maybe Bin Laden didn't actually hate Shakespeare's Stratford quite that much back then, but is now convincing himself that he did. It would match his mother's conviction that he was only radicalised when he went to university.[7] Memories, at the end of the day, can place disproportionate weight on specific moments to create a justifiable life narrative; this may or may not be conscious. An adult may retrieve and encode certain childhood memories; in extreme cases, this can lead to deliberate misrepresentation or even false memory. This is a particularly debated possibility in relation to negative events susceptible to repression and later retrieval.[8] There are several possibilities: a "source-monitoring error" (Bin Laden attributes this memory to dislike of Western society when this memory did not cause his dislike of Western society); "misinformation effect" (the information Bin Laden received between the memory and the recollection has made him link the memory to his dislike of Western society); "confabulation" (Bin Laden misinterprets this memory without any intention to deceive). Indeed, Bin Laden seems to be searching for hidden memory (disliking the West while at the birthplace) behind the overt memory (actually visiting the birthplace) – and he seems keen to emphasise the former despite the latter being more clearly factual. Whatever the case, Bin Laden appears to be retrieving and encoding his memory. Many psychologists have linked memory with "attachment", particularly formative memories with attachment to parents or caregivers. It could be argued that by floating this memory, Bin Laden is activating his own sense of attachment to his current self as represented by his ideology and message.

In other words, while there is every chance that this was indeed a formative moment in his development, Bin Laden the adult *needs* to dislike Shakespeare either way. It isn't all too different to sporting rivalries: allegiance can cease to be a choice and demands as much disassociation with the rival as association with one's own. In fact, increased disassociation can be the strongest way to reinforce one's association; it's why the most passionate support is going to be on derby day. The al-Qaeda leader has no choice: he must hate what Shakespeare represents, and better yet, root it in and out of some kind of constructive narrative. What's more, in the ball game (let alone something like the Middle East conflict), the youngster abides by the socialisation and expectation that comes with the place he or she is affiliated with and the passionate love/hate the parents, sat in the next seat, are projecting towards their own/rival entity. Ours is a world in which, more often than we care to admit, we find meaning through binaries. That these binaries are often the result of social expectations raises questions about how much freedom we might actually possess. Come to think of it, do I, as a literary critic, have a choice but to admire Shakespeare? Is some part of us actually relieved that Bin Laden hated Shakespeare? Essentially, does Bin Laden have a choice but to hate Shakespeare? Indeed, as sociologist Charles Horton Cooley's early 1900s theory of the "looking glass self" contends, we can also develop our sense of self based on our perceptions of how others think of us (a concept complicated further by the ascent of social media). Or, more importantly, consider the resistant reader in literary reception: one who consciously positions themselves in opposition to the expected views of a text. As important as resistant reading can be for underrepresented and oppressed groups, one could argue that even that reader might abide by a characteristic expectation to resist normative readings in order that they can champion, for instance, a feminist or politicised perception. We will return to resistant reading in the first chapter. In the conclusion to this book, I shall also reflect on what I term *resistant reception*, as well as my theorisations about the impact of the *entry point* and *periphery neglect* on literary reception.

"I have read most of works by #Shakespeare and enjoyed them" [*sic*]. Iran's Supreme Leader, the Grand Ayatollah Khamenei, tweeted this celebration of Shakespeare on 24 April 2016, commemorating the 400th anniversary of Shakespeare's death (23 April 1616). That Khamenei missed the anniversary by a day is less interesting than the fact that his account tweeted this at all. You see, the Ayatollah is supposed to be all-knowing, so he, too, has no choice: he must give the impression that he knows his Shakespeare. He does so via the same social media account he uses to deny the Holocaust every now and then. We shall return to Khamenei and Iran in the next chapter, but the tweet is an apt, almost exaggerated demonstration of the way in which expectations can govern and limit the freedom with which we fashion and engage our opinions and in turn, how we formulate our individual or collective identities.

While the recent surge in identity politics has brought important issues to the fore, there remains a risk that when it goes wrong, polarisation only furthers. Granted, Kimberlé Crenshaw's vital views on intersected identity categories can create positive change: "Drawing from the strength of shared experience, women have recognized that the political demands of millions speak more powerfully than the pleas of a few isolated". This comes with an obvious caveat: that black and white women "nevertheless experience ... oppressive power differently".[9] Indeed, incumbent economy- and defence-driven capitalist models of power, much like bourgeois nationalism in Marxist theory, will inevitably create hierarchies (of class, race, and so on), thus intensifying the gaps in society, or as some might put it, "dividing and ruling". In such a context, done wrong, identity politics can fall into the trap of upholding a manifesto of division. For Bin Laden, as for most people, identity can – consciously or not – be as much about what we are as what we are not.

This is emphasised further when one's identity is under attack. The Arab region, for instance, to which much of the recent Western concerns with terror relate, underwent periods of colonisation and war as well as authoritarian rule by autocrats, Islamists, militaries, monarchies, and communists. At each stage, some identities were threatened so defined themselves through what they rejected. The next chapter will link this aspect of identity to Shakespeare and terror more thoroughly, but what is becoming clearer is that Bin Laden's journal entry is significant in that it relates to a perception of his own identity, whether formative, retrospective, or both.

Why dislike Shakespeare? In the BBC's period sitcom *Blackadder*, the repeated Shakespeare motifs are no real surprise. In the follow-up finale movie, *Blackadder: Back & Forth* (1999), when Lord Blackadder (Rowan Atkinson) travels back in time, he literally bumps into Shakespeare (Colin Firth) and they begin to gather the manuscript pages that have been dropped. After Blackadder gets Shakespeare's autograph on the frontispiece of *Macbeth*, he precipitously punches the playwright to the floor: "That is for every schoolboy and schoolgirl for the next four hundred years". I recall watching this in a history class at school one Christmas (probably about the same age as Bin Laden was when he visited Stratford); Shakespeare's knockout fall to the ground was met by an uproar of cheering in the classroom, celebratory arms raised in the air. Freedom from what is imposed on us is a common desire.

One of the prices that Shakespeare continues to pay for his iconic status is that he becomes a part of hegemonic culture. Without adhering to the existence of definite ideological state apparatus or absolute historicism, one can still see that Shakespeare's presence in education systems worldwide, as well as popular media and culture, can certainly position him within a hegemonic paradigm that upholds dominant cultures and systems. Similarly to how oppressed groups have often positioned themselves as resistant readers of literature, rejecting Shakespeare in particular can be a way of freeing or differentiating oneself from commonly accepted or imposed norms – something which, as we'll see, many terrorists want to do. The irony is that freedom to interpret identity can result in adhering to one that is equally socialised or imposed.

Imran Awan, a leading UK criminologist, categorises the routes to radicalisation as comprising either push or pull factors. Push factors involve a feeling of "retribution" or "grievance" against something or someone. Pull factors involve being lured for a supposedly greater cause because the person is, for instance, unemployed, feeling neglected, or does not have a sense of belonging. This terrorist will see a romanticised image of a brotherhood or cause which pulls them in. In this process, identity becomes increasingly important, though this identity can be imposed by the ideologists and propagandists of that cause. Succumbing to pull factors, by no coincidence, relates to identity: wanting a sense of belonging or the feeling of a group dynamic, trying to be distinct from the crowd, backing an "us versus them" mentality, or displaying one's hyper-masculinity.[10] These routes to radicalisation involve the person seeking an individual or collective identity. As Awan notes: "Pull factors are stronger because they shape the person, the character". He notes that someone like Shamima Begum – the much reported British teenager who fled to the so-called Islamic State (ISIS) in Syria and some years later, decided she wants to return to the UK before having her citizenship revoked – was never likely to be accepted back because she was pulled more than pushed into ISIS. "If Begum had been pushed – if she has a grievance – you can de-radicalise somebody or de-programme them", explains Awan. "But the government is thinking that she can't be deprogrammed because she's gone too far down the pulled route", or in other words, she sought and reshaped an identity. I contend, then, that identity is pivotal to the extremist mindset: they try to uphold an identity they think has been quashed or to seek a newer, aspired identity. I also contend that the push and pull factors most often link to aspects of freedom. On push factors, a grievance can involve somebody taking something away, like one's land, one's loved one, or of course one's sense of identity. On pull factors, which are more proactive, wanting a sense of belonging involves attempting to free oneself from an imposed group; trying to be distinct from the crowd involves attempting to free oneself from a hegemonic, repetitive existence, and so on. Awan, who has studied terrorist mentality for years, adds that they have "external" and "internal" aims. Some terrorists seek "literal freedom from oppression or dictatorship", but "from a psychological or psychodynamic perspective, there is also an internal sense of trying to escape something".

The dangers associated with perceived freedom become even stronger if paralleled with the rise of such ideas as anti-intellectualism, a phenomenon social scientists have yet to link closely enough with extremism. One could argue that anti-intellectualism is an escape from the impositions associated with believing the intellectuals, but inadvertently leads to following an even more clearly imposed populist opinion that, unlike scholarly debate, does not always leave room for subtlety. The binary perception of anti-intellectualism aligns with some terroristic mindsets. Rather than accept authoritative opinion, they choose to believe that this opinion is purposely formulated to undermine their cause. It is no coincidence that so many alt-right members dispute the official immigration figures (which are lower than their narrative implies) and deny the existence of such scientific realities as climate change. Acceptance of these facts would reduce the authority of populists or manipulators. Their pseudo-nostalgic force is powerful – and it plays at the intersection of identity and freedom. For example, the alt-right terrorist longs for a nostalgic, imperial past, apparently void of multicultural societies and global citizenship. The religiously fanatic terrorist idealises a distant religious utopia of the past and frowns on the Islamic concept of tajdīd, meaning renewal. Renewal was a key component of the nineteenth-century push by modernist Islamic thinkers for ijtihād (diligence, implying independent reasoning and innovation) in relation to previously held details pertaining to the faith. But the fact that every authoritative Islamic scholar today condemns ISIS does not make the terrorists think twice. Instead, for instance, they launched a propaganda film in 2017 called Kill the Apostate Imams, which called for the assassination of many authoritative Islamic scholars. Justifying their actions using long passed away scholars, out of context, adds irony: if they were alive today, these scholars would also condemn ISIS. This mentality is in theoretical disagreement with Shakespeare, whose very canon shows opposition to anti-intellectualism. The playwright didn't oppose new creative or business ideas in the form of purpose-built theatres and utilisation of the printing press. He believed in reinvigoration: for the large part, he did not invent his plots from scratch, instead choosing to acknowledge and reinvent many existing sources.

Rather than exploring such links to present and pressing issues, literary studies have tended to utilise the current understanding of terrorism as a glass through which to see historical events contemporary to Shakespeare, not least the Gunpowder Plot.[11] In 1996, Garry Wills positioned *Macbeth* (as well as John Marston's *Sophonisba*, Thomas Dekker's *The Whore of Babylon*, and Barnabe Barnes's *The Devil's Charter*) as a Gunpowder play that responded to public interest in the event. He compares the play to movies about Pearl Harbor or the Kennedy Assassination (valid comparisons since 9/11, the more obvious event to link today, had yet to occur).[12] But studies on Shakespeare and terrorism tend to be historicist readings of the playwright as respondent to his contemporary events, post-terror. As a result, *Macbeth* is presented as an establishment response condemning the attempted Gunpowder Plot,[13] though some studies rightly complicate the straightforwardness of this perception.[14] Both sets of studies add to informative historical readings related to radical Elizabethan politics and in Shakespeare's case, enquiries about the extent of his political retorts and his Catholicism.[15] Most of these have appeared after 9/11, when interest in what literature and terrorism can elucidate about one another, not one but both ways, began to garner more serious interest. But the volume and relevance of such research remains minuscule in comparison to the vast influence of both literature and terrorism on how the world is shaped culturally, politically, and socially. One critic who has advanced the crossing is Peter C. Herman; he is quick to admit the fact that "literary scholars, however, have been surprisingly reluctant to deal with the topic".[16] Indeed, a less surprising drawback related to the topic is the sheer difficulty of defining terrorism, something even governments, NGOs, sociologists, and political scientists are having trouble with.

Defining terrorism, as Awan put it to me, is "the million dollar question". If it came to it, academics would debate it forever. It is a case in point that in the US alone, the FBI, Department of State, and the Department of Defense do not have a unifying definition. The FBI describes it as "unlawful", the Department of State as "premeditated", the Department of Defense as "calculated". Only the FBI mentions terrorism as involving "social" motives and only the Department of Defense mentions "ideological" motives. In the UK, the Crown Prosecution Service notes that terrorism "must also be for the purpose of advancing a political, religious, racial or ideological cause".[17] A legal definition is required, as noted by Ahmed al-Dawoody, Legal Adviser for the International Committee of the Red Cross in Geneva. In his book, he comments that

> specialists ... usually interpret the nature and root causes
> of terrorism from the perspective of the theories and
> methodologies of their disciplines and in so doing, in many

cases, they misrepresent the nature and causes of this
phenomenon.[18]

Al-Dawoody, the scholar turned legal specialist, makes a
convincing case for the pivotal position of context in even
attempting to define terrorism. In this way, the term becomes
fluid, rather than static (much like literary periods, theories,
and devices). While the difficulty with examining context is
its potential to shift or share blame for atrocities, al-Dawoody
backs his position by rejecting Susan Tiefenbrun's claim that
seeking to explain the root causes "would legitimize terrorist
acts".[19] He asserts that "this argument is flawed: knowing
and studying the motivations and causes of something does
not justify it. On the contrary, knowing the motivations of
terrorism is the first step to tackle it".[20] This notion of context is imperative to understanding the relationship between
Shakespeare and terrorism, whether the motivations of
terrorists responding to Shakespeare, or the motivations of
Shakespeare's terrorising or terrorised characters in the plays.
Terrorism, then, is linked to both the action and the motive.
The latter often carries disproportionate weight when events
are reported in media, condemned publicly, or go through
the juridical process. It is possible for someone to hijack
something or go on a killing spree for personal or pecu-
niary reasons. This has led to serious inconsistencies in media
coverage of terrorism. When the perpetrator is white, reports
are more likely to describe them as "lone wolves" rather
than terrorists, their actions as "mass shooting" rather than
domestic terrorism, and with disproportionate emphasis on
their mental issues that led to the attack. It is also possible for
someone to be convicted of terrorism without committing

any action (by plotting, inciting, or even failing to report one).[21]

Perhaps, then, rather than attempting to gather or deliberate definitions of terrorism within such tight confines, we are better off considering its contextual relation to such issues as identity, freedom, and the binary oppositions that these bring to the fore. I have already touched on the idea that defining one's identity is often stimulated by a search for freedom from the perceived shackles of another unsought identity. This notion links clearly to the rhetoric surrounding terror today, as al-Dawoody's discussion indicates:

> it is "comfortable" for each party to a conflict to blame the other party in general or the other party's religion for motivating acts of unjust war or terrorism because this makes each party feel psychologically that their religion and history are morally superior. Moreover, this relieves them of the psychological burden of belonging to the religion, culture, or nationality of the party convicted, or even merely controversially accused, of committing genocide or massacres – even if such atrocities were committed hundreds or thousands of years ago.[22]

There is an inextricable link between the phenomenon of terrorism and notions of identity, including non-identification. That's why, as the potent cliché goes, one person's terrorist will always and without fail be another's freedom fighter. Note that word again: freedom.

It is equally hard to define such an abstracted concept as freedom, particularly for those whose liberties have never really been purged. Freedom therefore becomes *symbolised* through various identifications and non-identifications. And terrorism becomes first and foremost an act of symbolism. It is hugely concerned with spectacle. Much as Shakespeare can symbolise certain idealised values, Guy Fawkes and Bin Laden have become symbolic of particular positions, oppositions, and events. The Gunpowder Plot failed, the attack on a theatre playing *Twelfth Night* in Qatar killed only the director (and the attacker), 3,000 people were killed on 9/11. But the event itself may not be as important as its symbolism. In the case of 9/11, attacking the heart of the US system made it ultimately more effective and consequential in the shorter and longer term. The footage of 9/11 embedded stark imagery into people's minds, making its symbolism monumentally stronger than if it was reported only in text. Again, recalling his studies of terrorist mentality, Awan notes that "in some cases, it has been about trying to kill as many people as you can, but often, it doesn't matter how many people are killed because it's the symbol behind what they are doing that counts". Terrorism is damaging, but first and foremost, it is symbolic.

The symbolism is significant and layered. In 2019, the FBI charged a twenty-three-year-old neo-Nazi, Conor Climo, with plotting to bomb a synagogue and a night club in Las Vegas. It soon transpired that Climo was being supported by the Baltic-based Feuerkrieg Division (FKD), a splinter of the violent white supremacists, the US-based terrorist organisation Atomwaffen Division (AWD), whom the FBI describes as "challenging the established laws, social order, and government via terrorism and other violent acts". Many of its members have been arrested for carrying out or plotting similar attacks, particularly on Jews, including links to the Pittsburgh synagogue shooting in 2018. The FKD's online posts include a shocking image of a screenshot from an ISIS video about making homemade explosives, with the caption "It's easier than you think". Equally disturbing is the AWD's propaganda, with one image featuring a stylised portrait of none other than Bin Laden himself, accompanied by his reported quote: "When people see a strong horse and a weak horse, by nature, they will like the strong horse". These neo-Nazi networks not only use propaganda related to both al-Qaeda and ISIS, but are now calling for "emulation" of these groups while bluntly idolising Bin Laden for his violent anti-authoritarianism and his front-page reach.[23] Terrorist groups who, on the face of it, believe in different things, can inspire one another. If we need confirmation that terrorism – in this case manifested through 9/11 and Bin Laden – holds symbolic weight on both sides of the spectrum, this neo-Nazi propaganda is as clear as it gets. And much as the symbolism terror propagates is so polarising – "horror" for most but "courage" for some (Macbeth 2.3.37; 1.7.60) – so too, can Shakespeare be symbolic and polarising.

What these groups do have in common is a shared articulation of terror. There are many types of terrorism, from dissident to state-sponsored, as well as political, religious, and criminal terrorism. Often, these overlap, and all seem to propagate an ideology. On every side, we appear to end up with a battle of ideological propagation, most often involving some concept of freedom. Even countering terrorism can propagate its own ideology of freedom (for example, from patriarchy in Afghanistan or dictatorship in Iraq).

In this book, terrorism is considered in those terms: dissident, state-sponsored, religious, criminal – but given the difficulty of categorising individual contexts and events, the type is not necessarily stated. Instead, the examples will show aspects of terror being inflicted by or on an individual or group. Indeed, there is also understandable traction building that the term "terrorist" should be avoided due to the fact that its frameworks and methods are grounded in Islamophobic, orientalist, and anti-black paradigms and prejudices. This book does not have the scope to explore this issue but is equally uncomfortable about ignoring these criticisms of the terminology. Though the book uses the term, it attempts to do so consistently and with an awareness of the multiple meanings and insinuations at play.[24] It is a shame that previous research on Shakespeare and terrorism has not been so careful. For instance, terms like "Islamic terrorism" have been used readily without appreciating key discussions in the social sciences.[25] In a vitally important article on the language of the debate, Richard Jackson explains how terrorism "has emerged as one of the most important political discourses of the modern era" and notes the "deeply problematic notion of 'Islamic terrorism', a term that comes laden with its own set of unacknowledged assumptions and embedded political-cultural narratives". On this term, Jackson's research "concludes that the discourse of 'Islamic terrorism' is profoundly unhelpful" as it is, first, "predicated on a number of highly problematic and contestable labels, assumptions and narratives", and second, it "functions politically to naturalize and legitimize particular forms of knowledge and political practices".[26] Today, the phrase even serves as a right-wing shibboleth (Donald Trump used it repeatedly to differentiate himself from and criticise the more nuanced approach of his predecessors), one not fundamentally separable from the shibboleth of "Western civilization" to which Shakespeare's name is sometimes annexed.[27]

***

The present book has a double focus on both the past and present. In many ways, it serves as a cultural history. It gives as much importance to presentism as historicism. Its rationale stems from two underlying questions. What can Shakespeare's life and works tell us about terrorism? And what does terrorism, as motive or action, tell us about Shakespeare's life and works? To get closer to the answer, I will be concerned with how and why terrorists have responded to Shakespeare – whether they've hated him or loved him. I will also observe and interrogate events, characters, and themes related to Shakespeare and his works in order to show their links to terror. On one hand, the book presents an alternative study of some famous terroristic events and figures, and on another, it presents surprising readings about the playwright and his plays that can make us consider their multifaceted content and presence anew.

The upcoming chapters advance the argument of this introduction, emphasising how identity, freedom, and symbolism are in a state of interplay. The first and most substantial chapter – "'Danger from the east unto the west': the tragedy of comedy" – is concerned predominantly with reception of Shakespeare in Muslim-majority countries, including terror attacks and extremist responses related to Shakespeare. Travelling through Afghanistan, Algeria, Egypt, Iran, and Qatar, it paints an unexpected image of the links between Shakespeare on one hand and political events and social ideas on the other. It also proves how approaching the reception of Shakespeare involves a wider lens that covers cultural history. Noting the first chapter's focus on reception of the work as opposed to the text, the second chapter – "'To me it is a prison': freedom and principled violence" – switches its attention to *Hamlet* and in particular to the character of the protagonist. It contends that approaching Shakespeare from a new entry point that is both atmospheric and related to social scientific definitions can challenge the most commonly held assumptions about the play. In particular, reading Hamlet's actions and words in light of terrorist psychology suggests a character who is at once more complicated and more simple than we assume: one who fixates on different types of freedom, nostalgia, and religious ideology to justify his violence. Whereas the opening examples of reception predominantly examined instances of indignation with Shakespeare, the third chapter – "'Though this be madness, yet there is method in it': performing ideology and power" – considers examples of how Shakespeare's plays have been utilised by terrorists to justify extremist ideology and its symbolic spectacle. In addition to examples that shed light on East-West relations and Shakespeare's utilisation in Nazi Germany, the chapter uncovers the story of the swastika flag that flew over Shakespeare's birthplace in 1939. The final chapter – "'As he was ambitious, I slew him': identity and assassination" – focuses on how, in the wrong hands, Shakespeare can be used to fatal ends and can inspire assassination. It also looks at the context surrounding the Gunpowder Plot to assess how this playwright from a small town in the British Midlands felt equipped to construct and enter the minds of characters so careless of consequence and so imbued with a mission that they were ready to sacrifice everything. This introduction has noted how Bin Laden's dialogues could have been, to some extent, staged and scripted. Can we say, then, that in his final days, he himself played the role of playwright (an unwilling double of what he detests)? And so, the afterword to the book will ask a question that looms large throughout: one about our own roles in all of this. To what extent does life imitate art?

NOTES

1 Walter Raleigh, "Shakespeare and England", in *England and the War* (Teddington: Echo Library, 2007).

2 All quotations from Shakespeare's plays and poems are from *Complete Works*, ed. Jonathan Bate and Eric Rasmussen (Basingstoke: RSC/ Macmillan, 2008).

3 On different types of fear in Shakespeare, see Robert Appelbaum, "Shakespeare and the Concepts of Fear", *Actes des congrès de la Société française Shakespeare* 36 (2018).

4 Panee Wongthienthong, "Movie Ban due to 'Climate of Fear'", *Bangkok Post* (18 April 2012).

5 "Full Text of Tony Blair's Foreword to the Dossier on Iraq", *The Guardian* (24 September 2002), www.theguardian.com/world/2002/sep/24/ iraq.speeches [accessed 9 September 2019].

6 Zbigniew Brzezinski, "Terrorized by 'War on Terror'", *Washington Post* (25 March 2007).

7 Martin Chulov, "My Son, Osama: The al-Qaida Leader's Mother Speaks for the First Time", *The Guardian* (3 August 2018), www.theguardian. com/world/2018/aug/03/osama-bin-laden-mother-speaks-out-family-interview [accessed 9 September 2019].

8 Both Pierre Janet and Sigmund Freud were interested in "false memory". Psychotherapists and memory researchers have since engaged in the "Recovered/False Memory debate" and the issues associated with different memory recovery techniques. For a summary, see Daniel B. Wright, James Ost, and Christopher C. French, "Recovered and False Memories", *The Psychologist* 19.6 (2006): 352–55, and Martin Conway, ed. *Recovered Memories and False Memories* (Oxford: Oxford University Press, 1997). In 1993, the British False Memory Society was established "to raise public awareness of the inherent dangers of false memory"; see http://bfms.org.uk/about/ [accessed 9 September 2019].

9 Kimberlé Crenshaw, "Mapping the Margins: Intersectionality, Identity Politics, and Violence against Women of Color", *Stanford Law Review* 43.6 (1991): 1241–99, 1241, 1280.

10 Imran Awan, in conversation with Islam Issa (October 2019), unless otherwise stated.

11 For example, Robert Appelbaum, *Terrorism before the Letter: Mythography and Political Violence in England, Scotland, and France 1559–1642*

(Oxford: Oxford University Press, 2016); Robert Appelbaum, "Early Modern Terrorism", in *Critical Concepts: Terrorism*, ed. Peter C. Herman (Cambridge: Cambridge University Press, 2018), 36–52.

12 Garry Wills, *Witches & Jesuits: Shakespeare's "Macbeth"* (New York: Oxford University Press, 1996). See also Robert Appelbaum, "Shakespeare and Terrorism", *Criticism* 57.1 (2015): 23–45; Peter C. Herman, "'A Deed without a Name': *Macbeth*, the Gunpowder Plot, and Terrorism", *Journal for Cultural Research* 18.2 (2014): 114–31.

13 Francis Barker, *The Culture of Violence: Essays on Tragedy and History* (Chicago: University of Chicago Press, 1993); Graham Holderness and Bryan Loughrey, "Shakespeare and Terror", in *Shakespeare after 9/11: How a Social Trauma Reshapes Interpretation*, ed. Matthew Biberman and Julia Reinhard Lupton, Publication of Shakespeare Yearbook 20 (Lewiston: Edwin Mellen, 2011), 23–56.

14 Alan Sinfield, *Faultlines: Cultural Materialism and the Politics of Dissident Reading* (Oxford: Oxford University Press, 1992); Peter C. Herman, *Unspeakable: Literature and Terrorism from the Gunpowder Plot to 9/11* (New York: Routledge, 2019).

15 Recent works that have painted Shakespeare as a playwright who did question authority include: Rebecca Lemon, *Treason by Words: Literature, Law, and Rebellion in Shakespeare's England* (Ithaca: Cornell University Press, 2006); Richard Wilson, *Secret Shakespeare: Studies in Theatre, Religion and Resistance* (Manchester: Manchester University Press, 2004); Arthur F. Kinney, *Lies Like Truth: Shakespeare, Macbeth, and the Cultural Moment* (Detroit: Wayne State University Press, 2001); Peter Lake, *How Shakespeare Put Politics on the Stage: Power and Succession in the History Plays* (New Haven: Yale University Press, 2016); Stephen Greenblatt, *Tyrant: Shakespeare on Politics* (London: W. W. Norton, 2018); Chris Fitter, *Radical Shakespeare: Politics and Stagecraft in Early Modern England* (New York: Routledge, 2012); Chris Fitter, ed. *Shakespeare and the Politics of Commoners: Digesting the New Social History* (Oxford: Oxford University Press, 2017). On the Catholic question, see James Shapiro, *1606: Shakespeare and the Year of Lear* (London: Faber & Faber, 2015) and Stephen Greenblatt, *Will in the World: How Shakespeare Became Shakespeare* (London: W. W. Norton, 2004).

16 "Introduction: Terrorism and Literature", in *Critical Concepts: Terrorism*, ed. Peter C. Herman (Cambridge: Cambridge University Press, 2018), 1–15, 4.

17 Crown Prosecution Service, "Terrorism" (2017), www.cps.gov.uk/terrorism [accessed 9 September 2019].

18 Ahmed Al-Dawoody, *The Islamic Law of War: Justifications and Regulations* (New York: Palgrave Macmillan, 2011), 185.

19 Ibid.; Susan Tiefenbrun, "A Semiotic Approach to a Legal Definition of Terrorism", *ILSA Journal of International and Comparative Law* 9.2 (2002–2003): 357–89, 389.

20 Al-Dawoody, *The Islamic Law of War*, 279, note 246.

21 The UK's Crown Prosecution Service notes:

> It is important to note that in order to be convicted of a terrorism offence a person doesn't actually have to commit what could be considered a terrorist attack. Planning, assisting and even collecting information on how to commit terrorist acts are all crimes under British terrorism legislation.

It also has an FAQ, "Can someone be charged with a terrorism offence if they know someone is about to commit a terrorism offence and don't report them?", with the answer "Yes". On media coverage, see for instance, Caroline Mala Corbin, "Terrorists Are Always Muslim but Never White: At the Intersection of Critical Race Theory and Propaganda", *Fordham Law Review* 86.2 (2017): 456–85.

22 Al-Dawoody, *The Islamic Law of War*, 184.

23 Ben Makuch and Mack Lamoureux, "Neo-Nazis Are Glorifying Osama Bin Laden", *Vice* (17 September 2019), www.vice.com/en_us/article/bjwv4a/neo-nazis-are-glorifying-osama-bin-laden [accessed 9 September 2019].

24 The use of "terrorism" in the title alludes to the fact that this book deals with real-life political and social events and figures, not just thematic or abstract ideas of terror in the plays.

25 For example, Graham Holderness and Bryan Loughrey, "Shakespeare and Terror", and Graham Holderness, "Rudely Interrupted", in *Tales from Shakespeare: Creative Collisions* (Cambridge: Cambridge University Press, 2014), 207–25. The latter also includes questionable translations from Arabic to English.

26 Richard Jackson, "Constructing Enemies: 'Islamic Terrorism' in Political and Academic Discourse", *Government and Opposition* 42.3 (2007): 394–426, 394–95, 412.

27 On Trump's use of the phrase, see Peter Holley, "'Radical Islamic Terrorism': Three Words that Separate Trump from Most of Washington", *The Washington Post* (1 March 2017), www.washingtonpost.com/news/the-fix/wp/2017/02/28/radical-islamic-terrorism-three-words-that-separate-trump-from-most-of-washington/ [accessed 12 March 2021].

"Danger from the east unto the west"

The tragedy of comedy

One

IRAN: IDENTIFICATION AND RESISTANCE

There was once a time when a whole country agreed unanimously to give up smoking. Persia's Tobacco Protest of the early 1890s (in Farsi, the Tobacco Movement; in Arabic, the Tobacco Revolution) was one of the sparks that led to a series of changes culminating in the Islamic Republic of Iran in 1979. As the unpopularity of the Qajar dynasty amplified due to loss of Persian land, widespread corruption, and high personal spending, the central government crumpled and Persia was governed at provincial and communal levels. The monarchy had given foreign powers numerous concessions, including the vital tobacco industry – production, sale, and export – to the British. What ensued was a major protest by the *bazaris* (merchants), joined by the *ulema* (clerics), who garnered major support until it became a national movement. The involvement of the clerics was pivotal: it was the first time they had led a popular movement in this way. Smoking was so prevalent at this time that people even smoked in mosques. It was no small step, then, when the Grand Ayatollah Mirza Shirazi declared a *fatwa* (ruling) that tobacco is forbidden. The people obeyed. Everyone stopped smoking. The tobacco concession was cancelled and for the first time, the people had opposed the Qajars.

DOI: 10.4324/9780429320088-2

The king of Persia during this revolt, Naser ad-Din Shah, would be assassinated a few years later. The new ruler, Mozaffar ad-Din Shah (1853–1907), donned a moustache as extravagant as his spending. As Persia's financial state was worsening, he borrowed money from Russia to fund his royal tours of Europe. Protests broke out in 1905 leading to the Persian Constitutional Revolution (1905–1911) that changed the course of the country. In August 1906, the Shah succumbed to demands for the founding of a new constitutional parliament (the *Majiles*) that would limit the monarchy's power. He died just months later. His son, Mohammad Ali Shah, with the support of Britain and Russia, cancelled the constitution and dissolved parliament (Russian military even stormed the building). The Shah announced that the constitution was anti-Islamic and the pro-constitutional activists were arrested, many of them intellectuals and philosophers. Although it is often assumed that British influence didn't infiltrate Iran, this couldn't be much further from the truth. In 1941, for instance, British troops entered Iran to give power to the final Shah, Mohamed Reza Pahlavi, by deposing his father. The UK's relationship with Iran's politics has been obvious (if dubious) – and with the political influence comes a cultural one.

While French culture had more influence than English culture in nineteenth-century Iran, the Constitutional Revolution made Shakespeare take centre stage. The first Farsi translations of Shakespeare emerged towards the end of the nineteenth century, coinciding with this period. It has been noted that the "propensity for translating and performing Shakespeare plays was so strong during the Constitutional era (1905–1907), that this epoch is mentioned as 'Shakespeare era' or 'The Age of Shakespeare' ".[1] The surge Shakespeare had at this time is no surprise: the period and its events were influenced by many

Iranians educated in the West. For instance, Yussef Etessami (1874–1938), who became a member of the *Majiles* in 1909, translated Shakespeare into Farsi. His journal published parts of *A Midsummer Night's Dream* and *Macbeth* and what is thought to be the first "encyclopaedic" essay on Shakespeare in the language.[2]

Another activist educated in Europe was Mohammed Mosaddegh, a rising political star in his early twenties during the constitutional reforms. When he became prime minister in 1951, he would take the opposite course to the Qajars by nationalising the country's oil industry, much to the US and Britain's fury. The oil nationalisation project was unacceptable to Winston Churchill and Dwight Eisenhower: in 1953, the MI6 and CIA's aptly named Operation Boot reinstated the Shah's powers through a coup that swiftly removed and imprisoned Mosaddegh, Iran's democratically elected, liberal prime minister. In time, this would result in a mistrust of the US and UK and a nationwide movement to depose the Shah. The Iranian Revolution of 1979, also known as the Islamic Revolution, would lead to the founding of the Islamic Republic with the Grand Ayatollah Ruhollah Khomeini essentially at the helm. It also affected US politics directly: the takeover of the US embassy in Tehran would be a factor in Jimmy Carter's election loss to Ronald Reagan the following year.

In 2011, a production named *HamletIRAN* set Shakespeare's play in modern Iran to remind its US audience of their country's role in mapping Iran's current political context. This *Hamlet*, directed by the US-based Iranian, Mahmood Karimi-Hakak, commented not only on the political polarisation of Iran but also on the long-lasting implications of foreign intervention. Indeed, the play begins with a foreign force, the Norwegian Fortinbras, marching towards Denmark, and ends with his claiming "rights of memory in this kingdom" (5.2.342). In Karimi-Hakak's version, the toppled Ghost of Hamlet's father is none other than the deposed Mosaddegh, the man unfairly removed from power. Hamlet shows his mother images of this rightful, virtuous leader, contrasting it with an image of his questionable and corrupt uncle, Claudius. At that moment, representing Claudius, the face of the populist President Mahmoud Ahmadinejad appears on the giant screen. The long-lasting, negative implications of foreign intervention are made clear. Deposing the democratically elected liberal leader would result in a reactionary increase in anti-Western populism until a figure even more hostile to the US and its allies came to power. Ahmadinejad took the presidency in 2005, winning a second term in the widely disputed 2009 election.

This led to mass protests around Iran that lasted for eight months. Protesters, widely known as the Green Movement, were suppressed. The movement was seen by many as an attempt to create change in Iran without more foreign intervention. Open fire was used by the police and Parliamentary *Basij*, a volunteer militia established by Khomeini during the 1979 Revolution and one of the branches of the Islamic Revolutionary Guard Corps (which Ahmadinejad is rumoured to have joined around that time). The most famous incident in the 2009 protests would involve Neda Agha Soltan: a video of her being shot in the chest was captured on video and spread on the Internet. Protesters identified a government militiaman as the shooter; the government blamed the CIA and suggested that the BBC and CNN had fabricated the footage.[3] The face of the twenty-six-year-old became an icon of this uprising and of state terror. In this production, her photographs form the backdrop of the stage as Ophelia's suicide is announced (Figure 1.1), confirming how young, innocent women's lives can be cut short in contexts of convoluted political ambition.

Figure 1.1 Ophelia drowns, *HamletIRAN*, 2011 (Mahmood Karimi-Hakak).

Karimi-Hakak is very clear about how his *Hamlet* serves as an allegory:

> In placing *Hamlet* within the Green Movement, I defined the characters to resemble those within the struggle. Ophelia, much like Neda, is the *innocence lost*. Gertrude is the country (Iran) that has moved, because of lust and greed, from Mosadegh to Ahmadinejad, Polonius (the puppet master) is Khamenei, and Laertes, the leader of the thugs. By the end of play they all suffer, as I believe their Iranian counterparts will. [4]

In early 1999, while still in Iran, Karimi-Hakak had put on *A Midsummer Night's Dream* at the Freedom Museum in Tehran (Figure 1.2). To stage a play in Iran, it must be approved by the Ministry of Culture, after which the play is performed exclusively for the ministry's Performance Review Board. If it passes, the board appoints auditors to ensure the performances remain consistent. It had taken Karimi-Hakak years to get Shakespeare's comedy approved. The first step was passed as officials noted its genre: "comedy, with little similarities to the present society in Iran". [5] After an official observation run, the director recalls the following response:

> There is nothing offensive about the play, although your production style is unusual and not what is expected from Shakespeare. Shakespeare is serious and profound. Your production is gay and playful. Your actors jump all over the stage, doing acrobatic type movements like they are birds or monkeys. This may be OK for Western audiences, they are shallow and light-minded, but our people are Muslims. They are somber people who have suffered greatly. They

Figure 1.2 Oberon: "How canst thou thus for shame, Titania",
Midsummer Night's Dream, 1999 (Mahmood Karimi-Hakak).

have offered their fathers, sons, and brothers as martyrs for
Islam. They are not going to like this play, I am sure. It would
be best for you to have your actors move less, especially the
female actors. They should remain in one place and recite
the beautiful lines of this great playwright.[6]

While the less political nature of comedy was perceived to
be safer than tragedy at step one, the officials appear to take
issue with the comic genre since they have nonetheless come

to expect Shakespeare the tragedian. Like many, they also miss the political sides of the comedy, which as Peter C. Herman has elucidated, ask serious questions about authority and constitution.[7] Most obviously, the officials show objection to artistic freedom and open demonstrations of sexuality. But they simplify the difference in reception between Muslim and Western audiences to such an extent that it also becomes a note on genre. While "shallow and light-minded" Westerners can enjoy the comedies, Muslim audiences are apparently formed of "somber people who have suffered greatly" and will thus find it harder to laugh. Shakespeare's comedy is used to explain seemingly disparate value systems, much like Bin Laden's note on Shakespeare's link to the "morally loose society" of the West, and as we'll see shortly, Khamenei's perception of the plays. What is more, the suffering and martyrdom appear to insinuate a history of Western colonisation and interference, something which Shakespeare can easily denote. Despite this, the officials have a high regard for Shakespeare's person and writing which goes as far as romanticising him. Shakespeare's representation of a past value system and his very canonicity fit into a narrative of a traditional, conforming society.

One evening, as the approved *Midsummer Night's Dream* was about to begin, a member of the Office of Observation and Evaluation took to the stage to announce its cancellation. Some of the audience refused to leave until the Revolutionary Guard dispersed them and arrests were made. The next evening, the fourth public performance, members of the Revolutionary Guard were apparently scattered around the theatre. The director recalls approaching two of them as the play was about to start:

> Introducing myself, I bluntly asked them if they were there to kill anyone. I said, "I know you do not like this play, and

obviously have not come to see the production. And I know you are here to stop this performance, but what I do not know is who sent you and whether you have orders to kill".

He records their reply as follows:

The one who *owns* this country and its people is the Last Imam.[8] And in his absence, this country and everything in it, including the people, are *owned* by his designated representative on this earth, the Velayate Faghih [The Supreme Leader of Islamic Republic of Iran].

They began to shout at the "whores" and "infidels" on the stage to stop and for the audience to leave the "blasphemous" space. The director obliged: "I feared that at any moment this comedy would turn into a violent attack".[9] The show was terminated and legal action began. Karimi-Hakak was summoned to a komīte – a kind of police station for religious matters, run by Hezbollah on behalf of the Interior Ministry. He was eventually charged and prosecuted with *tajavoz be efat-e omumi* (along the lines of "violating public decency"), leading to his move to the US. Recalling the events, Karimi-Hakak describes "a terrorizing experience, not only for me, my family, the cast and crew, but even for some audience members who objected to the raid". He also recalls how he and some cast members received death threats. In a context of political assassinations, he may have got off lightly. In January 2000, the Iranian Ministry of Intelligence admitted to its role in what have been called the Chain Murders: the killing of dissident intellectuals, like literature professor Ahmad Tafazzoli (1937–1997), over the last decade or so of the millennium.

***

Religion and politics blend very apparently in Iran. The Shi'ite Muslim belief in *ismah* (infallibility) has led to a long tradition of following a single individual, whether local or national, for doctrinal rulings. The main religious authority was an ayatollah. But with the founding of the Islamic Republic, the lead ayatollah's role became the Supreme Leader of Iran: the most powerful man in the country, controlling the military, judicial system, and state media – perhaps even the president. What the infallible ayatollah says is vitally important, used for instance, to make policy. It is semi-divine. What the ayatollah says about Shakespeare, then, cannot be dismissed. Khamenei's comments about Shakespeare over the years have been turned into diagrams and videos by Iranian news agencies. If the Islamic Republic had its way, this wouldn't be an interpretation of Shakespeare, it would be *the* interpretation of Shakespeare. His tweet for the 400th anniversary of the playwright's death reads:

> I have read most of works by Shakespeare and enjoyed them. Plays by Shakespeare are historical stories that he has formed them beautifully and they see most of his works in accordance with "values". Shakespeare plays, such as "Merchant of Venice" or "Othello" are all in accordance with values, but western values. [*sic*]

Khamenei shows how we have accepted Shakespeare's place in the cultural canon, worldwide and forever, elsewhere saying: "I myself might have read most of Shakespeare's work, and felt great enjoyment, respect and admiration for him". The Ayatollah uses Shakespeare to show that he knows and is up to date with, well, everything. Religious authority is no longer built on knowledge of theology alone, and almost anything can be used or skewed to strengthen or justify a narrative. For example, Khamenei chooses to mention Shakespeare's potentially anti-Semitic *Merchant of Venice*. Khamenei also comments on the difficulties faced by Shakespeare's female characters. In *Othello*, he explains, a black man gets married to an aristocratic woman. Although Othello is apparently black and ugly, Desdemona still becomes inferior to him because she is a woman – "this symbolises the Western viewpoint about women, and what a terrible viewpoint it is". This is proof, he adds, that Iranian women should be grateful.

Khamenei makes two overarching generalisations about Shakespeare. First, he sees the playwright as a didactic instructor who possesses, to use the Farsi term, "*orzor arshi*" (moral values). Second, he sees Shakespeare as someone who writes "histories". Both of these appear to meet an agenda in that they bring a more subtle cultural feud to the fore, since Khamenei proceeds to call on Iranian writers to pen their own "history" so that they no longer need to rely on Shakespeare's. A self-determined counter-history would bring with it appropriate values, whereas Shakespeare's apparently promote Western morals. In this sense, Shakespeare ends up representing something similar to Khamenei as he did to Bin Laden.

This desire to introduce one's own versions of history and culture at the expense of another can be justified quite easily (and is not necessarily something to be frowned upon). It does, however, echo many other attempts in the country. It's why, to give an example, WhatsApp is banned but an Iranian-friendly app is available: Suroush, named after a Messenger Angel. But Khamenei's narrative also acknowledges another dynamic: that Shakespeare might actually be so powerful and significant that even the Supreme Leader has no choice but to show (and show off) an engagement with him.[10] If he can't be avoided then he must be utilised. This use of Shakespeare also highlights a wider story of home-forced talent in Iran. For instance, after the Islamic Revolution, numerous singers absconded to the US in fear that music would be banned (it was for a short while). The Iranian government responded by opening up a little and promoting singers who, believe it or not, copied the exact same voices and vocals as those who'd departed. The political consequences in Iran have constantly led to feelings of loss which Iranian identity (whether individual or governmental) has needed to navigate or negotiate. This hasn't been done by disregarding popular culture or global trends, but by a process of replication. Once something has proven its cultural or artistic weight, it is accepted but altered, whether it's an early modern English playwright, a contemporary pop singer – or even a nuclear programme. And this is no secret. The Islamic Republic developed a policy of "localisation" (*boomi sazi*), ensuring that Western models (most notably cultural and political) are adopted but adapted to Islamic values and principles. It really is that vague: rather handy to allow maximum room for manipulation. This formula, replicate plus contextualise, has shaped how literature, including Shakespeare, is perceived and taught: a suspicion that it encourages apparently secular values, but a simultaneous need for those in power to show that they understand the Western models that they are critiquing.

The surge in Shakespeare over the last century symbolises the constant conflict of defining and shaping Iranian identity that has gripped the country, extending beyond the birth of the Islamic Republic. In fact, the revolutions were themselves shaped by this same struggle. On the one hand, there are those who insist on a more secular or Western model, and on the other, there are those who propagate what the Republic now calls an "Iranian-Islamic" identity. These two forces have grown increasingly suspicious of one another and often view their ideas in opposition, leaving little room for reconciliation.

It's worth noting, though, that Khamenei represents different modes of literary reception to Bin Laden. They offer respective examples of *negotiated reception* and *oppositional reception*.[11] Whereas Khamenei accepts Shakespeare but negotiates aspects to match his thought, Bin Laden appears to oppose Shakespeare more downrightly. To add to this, while Khameneni uses *identification* with Shakespeare's work as a route towards *disidentification*, Bin Laden makes his disidentification more immediately clear. They share similar goals, but Khamenei's appears to be more thought through since disidentification allows one "to use the energies and pleasures of identification for resistive and subversive ends".[12] Their responses indicate the ways in which, in literary reception, identification and disidentification can be powerful tools: here, they are catalysts for a wider, subversive form of messaging. Disidentification and negotiated/oppositional reception have often been viewed as empowering tools for underrepresented groups. But these two examples show that individual and collective expectations can dictate the nature of reception for the (dis)identifying recipient, in turn posing questions about freedom of interpretation.

Moreover, these examples raise questions about subordination and resistance as obvious dichotomies of reception. Literary reception theorists have appreciated how readers can subordinate themselves to a text in order to accept and receive it with some (potentially positive) level of passivity. But this *subordination* is most often considered in relation to a specific work, like a text or painting. And importantly, subordination is regarded as oppositional to *resistance*. I propose here that subordination can increase resistance. By appreciating Shakespeare's importance, Khamenei (and to some extent Bin Laden) subordinate to the playwright's cultural and canonical position – but not to Shakespeare's actual works. By subordinating to the cultural phenomenon (which carries more weight than an actual text), they are able to accentuate their resistance to what the work represents and comprises. This resistance inflates their own importance and bold capacity to challenge Western canonicity.

Moreover, I also contend that in addition to resistant reading (of a text), there is such a thing as *resistant reception* (of a work).

Resistant reading pays attention to the world of the literature by reading in opposition to the normative expectation, which can include, for instance, sympathy for the male, white, or European character and antipathy to the female, black, or orientalised character (in Shakespeare, resistant reading of *The Tempest* would be an attempt to feel sympathy for Caliban and antipathy to Prospero). And *resistant reception* speaks to this same challenge both inside and outside the world of the fiction. It links the work to wider issues of cultural hegemony and hierarchy as well as the multifaceted intersections of the reader's identity and experiences, in order to confront, for instance, a culture's perceived dominance or a writer's nonchalant canonicity. In turn, *resistant reception* can be a path towards more effective and holistic notions of resistant reading. I shall reflect further on this phenomenon, as well as my related theorisations of the *entry point* and *periphery neglect*, in the book's epilogue.

Returning to Bin Laden, while he does show some resistance, one shouldn't mistake this for a form of ignorance. His journal entries – and the list of books in his library released by the CIA – suggest a man who is well-read. The poetic verses beginning and ending his notebook and the general peppering of poetry every few pages are telling. The classified application form to join al-Qaeda asks such questions as whether the candidate prefers "literature" or "science", whether their educational background is "literary" or "scientific", as well as a less reasonable tick-box question about whether they are prepared to become a martyr and who should be contacted in that event. But literature clearly plays a part in terroristic thinking and in what makes a terrorist.

Khamenei's approach is a telling change from his predecessor, Ayatollah Khomeini, who, asked in 1979 about European composers such as Johann Bach and Ludwig van Beethoven, replied "I do not know those names".[13] With such context, it becomes less surprising that in 1989 Khomeini issued that infamous call for the assassination of Salman Rushdie following authorship of the controversial novel *The Satanic Verses*.[14] It is still in place and Khamenei in fact reaffirmed it in 2005. The publication had led to protests, as well as attacks on bookstores, publishers, and translators. The events had varying impacts. Perhaps for the first time, many global Muslims and specifically many British Muslims had a common, publicly visible profile and cause which affirmed, for better or for worse, a disparate identity. Indeed, the fault line of identity became more clearly divided on the basis of culture, and in fact, literature. The principles and extents of free speech were also put into question, something which has continued through today in relation to hate speech and racism.

THE ARAB WORLD: INTERVENTION AND DEMARCATION

It's a Saturday night in March 2005. A sudden, loud bang literally hurls a clown off the stage. It's Feste, on stage in

Doha for a performance of *Twelfth Night*. A man has targeted the theatre, mid-performance, with an explosive device.[15] Shakespeare's plays are admired for their subtle shifts from comedy to tragedy and vice versa. On that day, comedy suddenly became tragedy. Here, we ask some key questions: why did this terrorist have a problem with Shakespeare, and just what does this attack on Shakespeare elucidate in terms of history and culture? I will consider how Shakespeare's links with this event help to explain issues of colonialism and foreign policy, the symbolic nature of terrorism, and the fluctuating nature of Arab identity.

The attacker, inspired by al-Qaeda, was ready to drive his car – and the explosive device – directly into the Doha Players Theatre. But his car had trouble moving up the steps of the theatre, causing him to step on the accelerator, making a loud revving sound. The director of the play, a British teacher named Jonathan Adams, heard the noise and made his way out to check the commotion. At that moment, the attacker detonated his device, killing both him and the director. The roof collapsed and fire swept through the building. At least twelve members of the audience were injured, half of whom were Qatari nationals.[16] The community was shaken but has since come closer together; but they are also keen not to let the events define them.[17]

So, why attack a performance of Shakespeare? European literature has long been resisted (and accepted) in different ways across the Arab region. The Doha attack is a reminder that foreign policy may have replaced colonialism as the issue of indignation at hand. After all, its timing was precisely at the two-year anniversary of the invasion of Iraq. Over the last decades, Qatar has famously housed US army bases, including the Central Command, and this military presence is quite visible.

But to understand specific resistance to Shakespeare more fully, we might take some steps back. The British ruled Egypt – the key political, geographic, and cultural hub of the region – from the Anglo-Egyptian War of 1882 until the final British troops departed in 1956. In nineteenth- and twentieth-century Egypt, then, resistance to Shakespeare was resistance to British colonialism. While science was translated in the eighteenth and nineteenth centuries, literature wasn't, particularly as countries attempted to ratify Arabic as their official language. Colonialism meant Arabs felt a need to learn, preserve, and protect their identity through language and culture.

Modern Egyptian history is full of British influence. The British military invaded Egypt, still part of the Ottoman Empire, in 1882. When the First World War began in 1914, Britain declared Egypt a protectorate. The Revolution of 1919 involved widespread protests against the British, who tried to conclude a treaty that maintained their control of the Suez Canal. This didn't work, so in 1921, Britain imposed martial law in Egypt, leading to further fervent nationalism, and from 1922, Egyptian independence resulting in the creation of the Kingdom of Egypt. But in reality, the British remained in control and many saw the monarchy as puppets of the British. As nationalist discontent increased, the Revolution of 1952 would remove the monarchy and lead to the Republic of Egypt. The Muslim Brotherhood had played a pivotal part, through their anti-colonial (and therefore anti-monarchical) social mobilisation, including such figures as Sayyid Qutb, to whom we shall return. The General Muhammad Naguib and Lieutenant Colonel Gamal Abdel Nasser led the coup. Naguib, sympathetic to the Brotherhood, became first president, but was swiftly removed from power by Nasser, who also outlawed the group. The Muslim Brotherhood were accused of attempting to assassinate Nasser later in 1954, leading to the arrest and eventual execution of leading figures, including Qutb.

Rooted in colonialism, but sparking from opposition to the Egyptian monarchy and then to Nasser's hard socialism, two social movements would emerge and unexpectedly change Shakespeare's presence forever: from the nineteenth century, the cultural *nahdah* (renaissance), and from the mid-twentieth century, the Islamic *sahwah* (awakening). The *nahdah*, which was also influenced heavily by Lebanon and Syria, involved elevating Arabic literature through exploring its new potentialities for the purpose of cultural renewal and autonomy. In doing so, it was also keen to engage with foreign literature to show its ability to learn from and compete with it. It "expressed a dialectical desire for both cultural autonomy and to be part of world culture, though on the basis of that autonomy".[18] The *nahdah* was also linked directly with religious, national, and anti-imperialist fervour; much poetry at the time was anti-colonial, often advocating political Islamic identity. This deepened the national pride of this renaissance and would also help elevate the Islamic *sahwah*, which began as a social movement relying on common aspirations to develop the country.[19] When translations of Shakespeare finally appeared, then, they served ulterior and somewhat ironic motives. First, on the basis of the *nahdah*, to update the functions and capabilities of Arabic literature – by alluding and responding to the global canon. Second, on the basis of the *sahwah*, to intensify the morality of Egyptian theatre – by steering it away from increasingly comic and burlesque emphases.

Similarly but with different consequences, the introduction of French as the official language of Algeria, including for education, meant that Algerians growing up in that period had to maintain their oral, Arabic traditions. These traditions would also aid them to keep their own version of events intact as the education system was altered. Rather ironically, my two visits to Algeria were on behalf of the UK Foreign Office to take part in public events and talks related to Shakespeare. I would learn a lot from my thought-provoking friend (and driver) Firas, a hunched man with a slight but obvious limp who prides himself on punctuality and proves that being cultured can be as important as being formally educated. Firas' mother is one of millions of Algerians educated in French, an Arab who cannot read or write Arabic. In fact, one of the respected Shakespeare scholars in the country told me, after we shared a podium at the national book festival, "In Arabic, I am illiterate". He said so in perfect, classical Arabic.

There's an important element that frames Algeria differently to Egypt: the nature of the colonisation was incomparable – the Maghreb countries endured a Frenchification and the stakes and losses were practically greater. Algeria was considered a part of France, not the usual protectorate or colony. It is known to Arabs as the "country of a million martyrs". In the first decade of an occupation that lasted from 1830 to 1962, French genocides killed around a third of the three million population.[20] The Algerian national anthem, *Qasaman* or *The Pledge*, which the revolutionary poet Moufdi Zakaria apparently wrote on a prison cell wall using his own blood, swears by an array of things that Algeria "should live", with one stanza addressing the colonisers directly:

O France!
Past is the time of palavers
We closed it as we close a book

O France!
The day to settle the accounts has come!
Prepare yourself! Here is our answer!
The verdict, our Revolution will return it
We are determined that Algeria should live,
So be our witness – be our witness – be our witness![21]

Algerian national identity, as represented by the anthem, relies on non-identification with the coloniser, and their sense of self-determination on actively recalling the revolt against French oppression. As recently as 2008, to put an end to any controversy, the Algerian Constitution declared the anthem's status "immutable" and its lyrics unchangeable.

A movement to bring English literature into Algerian consciousness, then, became somewhat self-explanatory: as a retaliation to French literature during a period when the two European literatures were in competition for the top spot. Shakespeare was less English writer and more non-French writer. Many of those who had excelled in the French education system (known as the évolués – literally and derogatively meaning "the evolved") went on to lead the independence movement against the French – a more accomplished version of Caliban's statement: "You taught me language, and my profit on't / Is, I know how to curse" (1.2.423–24). Algeria gained independence in 1962 – swiftly making Arabic the official language and Islam the state religion – and one result was a surge in theatre activity. Rather symbolically, *The Taming of the Shrew* was translated just months later – into Algerian-Arabic. Importantly, Mustapha Kasdarli's rendition was not in French or in the usual Classical or Egyptian Arabic, thus fitting with Algeria's Self-Determination referendum. The play was performed to packed crowds on the newly formed national stage. But the ensuing Algerian civil war in the 1990s would polarise society massively. The literary elite, including actors and directors, were seen as too liberal and thus targeted by religious extremists while theatres were shut down. One of two high profile actors in this milestone performance of *Taming* was Abdelkader Alloula (1939–1994). A few years later, Alloula wrote and produced a radio programme about Shakespeare and he would go on to become an influential playwright and director. In March 1994 (during the month of Ramadan), on his way to the Palace of Culture in the coastal city of Oran, Alloula became the victim of a targeted assassination by one of the militant groups.

The differing responses to Shakespeare in Egypt and Algeria are not too different to Khamenei and Bin Laden's respective acceptance and rejection of Shakespeare. Both serve wider purposes while linking significantly to identity. The Algerian Civil War is much too complex to summarise, but can be pinpointed to some key events and groups. The National Liberation Front (FLN) was highly influential in expelling the French and ruled the country until other parties were allowed to contest. While Islamic identity was important to the anti-colonial struggle, religion did not forefront the FLN's policies. But like Egypt's *nahdah* and *sahwah*, nationalist identity and religious identity often strengthen one another. The FLN's fight against France was seen as a religious obligation. When the FLN needed to strengthen support in the 1980s, they invited leading Egyptian clerics Mohammed al-Ghazali and Yusuf al-Qaradawi to Algeria. The two scholars, who had affiliations to the Muslim Brotherhood, brought with them strong elements of political Islam, as embodied through the *sahwah*. When the popular Islamic Salvation Front (SIF) became clear winners of the 1991 election, its result was cancelled immediately and the military took over. The SIF was banned and many members arrested, leading to a rise in Islamist guerrilla movements. Thousands of their members had already experienced fighting in Afghanistan when they joined the war effort against the Soviets in the 1980s.[22] The more secular middle class and left wing (to whom much of the literary elite belonged) were among the groups targeted due to their general support of the military against the religious movements. The other targets included Muslims who refused to endorse the violent tactics, including the Algerian wing of Hamas, whom the Islamists considered too moderate (executing their leader in 1993). Tens of thousands died in the "Black Decade" that followed. But there were retaliations and losses on all sides during this time. While the attacks by the Islamist factions are well-known, records have revealed that the institutional apparatus and army also carried out attacks on civilians.[23] Again, identity became an issue of a more binary non-identification. For Algerians during the occupation and its recovery period, Shakespeare was one of them: not French. When the battle became framed as Muslim versus secular, to the Islamists, Shakespeare was no longer one of them.

In the case of Qatar, then, the presence of US military, Western migrants, and in fact Shakespeare performances, all come to symbolise foreign intervention, even invasion. Criminologist Imran Awan's research on the mindset of terrorists concludes that they "aren't maniacs" but highly "calculated". The significance of the target is always considered and generates what Awan calls "a ripple effect", creating fear, "so when you're on a train, for example, it's on the back of your head". Take, for instance, Bin Laden's little known relationship with soccer. He was allegedly a keen supporter of the London-based club

Arsenal. In March and April 1994, he went to the Highbury Stadium to attend two European Cup Winners' Cup matches and even made purchases at the club store. A couple of years later, he would head to Afghanistan. More relevantly, one of Bin Laden's first targets was actually the 1998 World Cup in France, a plot uncovered and foiled just in time. It is telling that this al-Qaeda plot on French soil, which Bin Laden is thought to have approved personally, was a joint operation with the Algerian Armed Islamic Group (GIA), one of the two main groups that was fighting against the Algerian army in the civil war and now affiliated with al-Qaeda. The plot in France included attacking the hotel hosting the US national team as well as killing England's players and fans during their match against Tunisia (ironically, given England's opposition in the game, many Muslims could have been victims). That this was Bin Laden's first serious plot in Europe is enormously telling given the symbolism of the World Cup as a global festival that is viewed by millions. That the targets were the US and England teams that represent these two countries confirms the nested symbolism of the target. Later that year, the next al-Qaeda plot would target the US embassies in Kenya and Tanzania – given that these embassies represent foreign presence and are de facto US soil, they are once more targets of symbolic significance. That attack was detrimental, killing over 200 people. But Bin Laden chose the less directly political but more symbolic World Cup plot first. In the case of the 2005 Qatar attack, then, al-Qaeda wanted to instil fear and make Westerners think twice before moving to the Gulf, and more specifically before transporting the British symbol of Shakespeare, through performing or attending the plays, into a Muslim-majority country.

***

The *sahwah* – and more recently and problematically, al-Qaeda – has long been linked with such figures as Sayyid Qutb, a founder of the Muslim Brotherhood who has since been regarded as an intellectual godfather and inspiration for political and radical Islam worldwide. Core elements of his writings have been used by extremist groups like al-Qaeda, including his support of an Islamic state and his hostility to the West, which he regarded "as the historic enemy of Islam and Muslims as demonstrated by the Crusades, European colonialism, and the Cold War".[24] Bin Laden's library included Qutb's books and both Khomeini and Khamenei admired the Egyptian, the latter even publishing Farsi translations of Qutb's works.

While imprisoned for a decade before his execution in 1964, and particularly in his final two years, Qutb formulated his main political philosophy which would go on to be interpreted dangerously by terrorists to drastic consequences. The tract, *Ma'ālim fi al-Ṭarīq* (*Milestones*), differentiates between Islam and *jāhiliyyah* (the state or time of ignorance, often referring to the pre-Islamic period in Arabia). In his view, the world returned to that ignorant state through secularism and dictatorship, whereas Islam offers the complete way of life. He called for a vanguard of Muslims to overcome the ignorance – through social action or force. The two options, as John Esposito indicates, are "evolution" or "revolution", the latter when the former is not possible.[25] In addition to being potentially inciting, some took Qutb's binary dichotomy as an excuse for *takfīr* (labelling someone as a disbeliever or apostate), something which is strongly discouraged in Islamic creed but actively encouraged by religious extremists.

Today, the term *jāhiliyyah* can be interpreted as a "system, ideology, or institution based on values other than those referring to God".[26] Qutb was concerned with the idea of utopia, which while linked to a religious state, requires social action and preaching of the faith (to those who identify as Muslims before non-Muslims) prior to any combat. As such, the extremist appropriation of Qutb takes his ideological viewpoint literally in very different contexts to his and without the possibility of either phasing or allegory. But he remains a popular figure in parts of the Arab world – as Esposito notes, one of the "martyrs as of Islamic revivalism".[27] And one could argue that, rather detrimentally, he "died before he could fully explain his theories".[28]

But Qutb wasn't just the face and spiritual leader of political Islam: he had spent time in influential literary circles, too, and wrote much literary criticism before his arrest. One might be justified to think that like those inspired by him, Qutb disliked Shakespeare. In fact, a Kuwaiti newspaper recently published an imagined interview with Qutb, in which a prominent Muslim Brotherhood thinker in the country visualises what Qutb would say. The columnist imagines a frustration that "Shakespeare has defeated Al-Mutanabbi (a prominent tenth-century Arabic poet) in our countries",[29] implying Qutb's combative relationship with the West. But it makes more sense to look at Qutb's regular contributions to al-Risālah, a major intellectual magazine that demonstrated the Arab nahdah.[30] His writing reveals something very different. In an article in May 1945, Qutb laments the government publisher's lacklustre approach to translating Shakespeare; they had cancelled a project that would render the plays in Arabic. Qutb concludes with hopes that one day "the Arab library can become a source of world culture".[31] In a book review, Qutb writes about Othello as an exemplar of how to depict "doubt", since "Shakespeare's energy" makes that aspect of the character convincing, something Arab writers would do well to learn from.[32] He also presents a positive reading of The Merchant of Venice, writing that a new Arabic play by Ali Ahmad Bakathir called The New Shylock is incomparable with Shakespeare's and not as successful at depicting "the inner Jewish soul" and its "plots and intrigues".[33] Read in line with his tract Our Struggle with the Jews, this anti-Semitic reading of Shakespeare is obviously problematic.

It is also clear that Qutb holds Shakespeare in high regard. This could be linked to a statement made by 'Umar ibn al-Khattāb (579–644), a key companion of Muhammad, who is reported to have said that "He who does not know al-jāhiliyyah (the state of ignorance) does not know Islam". If so, then similarly to Khamenei, Qutb is showing awareness of Western culture while confirming a more nuanced understanding of the benefits of non-Islamic cultures than his critics or the extremists inspired by him might imagine.

This seems to be a wider artistic interest on Qutb's part, as evidenced in his travel writings, also published in al-Risālah, as soon as he returned from the US, where he studied (including at Stanford) from 1948 to 1950. While at face value, his perceptions sound similar to Bin Laden's indignation at the incompatible value systems, Qutb's idea of taste is noticeable. Unlike the Taliban, who ban "American and British hairstyles", thus simultaneously confirming and refuting a globalised cultural hierarchy, Qutb is entirely confident about the superiority of his own taste. He notes how "anything that requires a touch of elegance is not for the American, even haircuts!" He recalls going home to "fix what the barber had ruined with his awful taste".[34] Qutb adds, "The American is primitive in his artistic tastes, whether in his judgment of art or his own artistic works", explaining that "cinema is the art of the masses". While this is usually cited to show his hostility to the West,[35] bringing in fuller context actually suggests Qutb's differentiation between high culture and low cultures. To Qutb, Hollywood movies "possess simplistic story lines and primitive emotions", unlike "brilliant films like 'Gone with the Wind,' 'Wuthering Heights,' 'Singing Bernadette,' [sic] and so on".[36] In praising the works of Margaret Mitchell, Emily Brontë, and Franz Werfel's novel about a Catholic saint, Qutb further undermines US popular culture but affirms an understanding of canonicity and even classicism. That he looks up to Shakespeare, then, is befitting. This consideration of Shakespeare's position poses a rather controversial but potentially expansive question: did the anti-Shakespearean members of al-Qaeda really understand Qutb?

Recently, an Islamic scholar, Fadel Suleiman, questioned how Qutb's reputation and selected works are being used by young terrorists to justify their actions. In an interview with an Egyptian newspaper, he used Shakespeare to explain this position:

> Imagine if the three [terrorists] said that Shakespeare's writings are what inspired them. Would you ban the writings of Shakespeare? Or would you convince the youth that they did not understand Shakespeare?[37]

The attack in Qatar emphasises the lasting effect of colonialism and foreign policy, as well as the symbolism of both Shakespeare and terror. But what more does the attack tell us? The al-Qaeda-inspired terrorist turned out to be an Egyptian man. Many Egyptians in Qatar – including members of my family – were deported in the weeks that followed. Aside from the practical struggles this generated, the attack on Shakespeare resulted in a further demarcation of Arab identity.

We might do well to start by remembering that the Arabian Peninsula wasn't always so many countries. The demarcation of Eastern Arabia (now Bahrain, Kuwait, Qatar, and parts of Iraq, Oman, and Saudi Arabia) left these individual countries trying to construct individual identities suited to the modern world's dominant views of heritage and identity. The Gulf wasn't always so rich either. The discovery of oil meant these countries had even more money to spend, not just on skyward construction, but on identity construction too.

The geography and politics of the region as we know it today is in large part the making of British geopolitical efforts. As World War One began, the Ottomans not only supported the Germans but also promoted pan-Islamism and held power in an economically attractive region. The Allies sought the support of various Arab factions, sparking the Arab Revolt against the Ottomans (1916–1918). Hussein bin Ali, the leader of Mecca, negotiated in secret with the British and French. He became king of Hejaz (a region of Saudi Arabia), with a grander aim of developing an Arab nation from Syria to Yemen that he could proclaim as a caliphate, with himself as caliph, obviously. The Allies agreed and promised Arab independence, but the deal was forsaken secretly in the Sykes-Picot Agreement that decreed, unbeknown to the Arabs, how the region would be split between the Allies. In the aftermath, the region came under European rule. When, in 1924, the Ottoman Caliphate was abolished and Hussein declared himself Caliph, the influential rival clan, the House of Saud, was quick to respond. Led by Abdulaziz ibn Saud, they attacked Hussein and his troops, ending 700 years of Hashemite rule (assumed descendants of Muhammad) in Mecca. The British, who'd supported Hussein, didn't step in to help their ally, who was exiled to east Jordan. In fact, Britain had started quiet diplomatic relations with ibn

Saud during the war. Britain would begin its continuing support to the Saud House, which took over the religious capitals of Mecca and Medina, and the important city of Jeddah (now the Kingdom's commercial capital). Two years later, Britain signed a treaty giving ibn Saud control of the region, leading to the birth of the Kingdom of Saudi Arabia.

Britain didn't attempt to export its culture into Saudi Arabia, knowing that the pact between the Saud clan (to do politics) and the Wahhab clan (to do religion) would clasp control of the region's population. The ideas of Muhammad ibn Abd al-Wahhab, who headed the latter clan, would develop into Wahhabism, an ultraconservative interpretation of Islam that has since been adopted by some terrorists. Shakespeare was only creeping into the region slowly during these periods and would be impeded further by heavy censorship, including self-censorship.

With the help of organised religion, the Gulf became a large gated community. Today, it is in some ways wide open, but contains smaller gated communities that represent worlds within worlds. Highly earning professionals don't want to live with construction workers so have their own compounds. In the wealthy Qatari district of Katara – between the skyscrapers of the West Bay and the luxurious artificial islands of The Pearl – a long road bears the name Shakespeare Street. The English playwright represents more in the country than that anomalous and callous attack. There is such obsession with security in Qatar that employees of the world's largest security company walk around the mosques donning mirrored aviator sunglasses and chewing vigorously at their cheeks. All of these factors make the attack on a theatre playing Shakespeare all the more striking.

And so, Shakespeare lives here in other ways: in a region where everything is commoditised, he cannot escape. The

Shakespeare and Co café-restaurant chain, founded in Dubai and now boasting tens of stores across the Gulf, is everyone's guaranteed point of contact with the playwright's name. "Every restaurant is distinctly 'Shakespearean'", the website boasts. There is very little – well, nothing but the name – that is Shakespearean about it. The décor is blindingly bright and exaggerated: its Englishness lost in a misreading of extravagant pseudo-vintage furniture. But in a world where value is associated with purchasing power and where size and glamour matter, this is an optimistic vision of the power of Shakespeare's name.

Unlike the dull, wooden taverns that Shakespeare would frequent, here, it must be a bright, shiny café in a world obsessed with artificial light. In 2016, NASA released the most detailed image of the world at night that showed a link between light and urban development. The Gulf is getting brighter and brighter: a symbol of creating a new, evolved identity in a place where emulation and possession are at the fore. The import of white migrant (usually called "expatriate", but never "immigrant") communities for lucrative jobs in the Gulf also serves to prolong the dominant hierarchies. So if the Gulf can't buy the Globe one day, they'll simply import it. This was most evident in 2017 when the Louvre opened in Abu Dhabi, costing almost $2 billion ($525 million for the name alone, plus $600 million to build and $750 million for the art). Both the inside (artworks) and outside (architecture) of the new Louvre confirm that the Gulf is not ready to present the world with its authentic historical culture or a new created culture, but as with everything else, it fetishises an ability to *purchase*, in this case, the dominant cultural capital. Attack or no attack, Shakespeare will remain a reliable name and symbol whose canonicity and hegemony can fill any perceived cultural vacuum.

AFGHANISTAN: WOMEN AND CONFLICT

In Afghanistan, one war followed another. The Soviet invasion from 1979 to 1989 resulted in a million civilian deaths and at five million people, one of the largest refugee outflows in modern history. It also meant that religious zeal – and combative *jihad* – became linked closely to nationalism. The ten-year war ended with the departure of the Soviets and an ensuing civil war. The Soviet-backed regimes fell by 1992 when the Mujahideen formed a government. From 1994, the Taliban rose to power. Led by Mullah Mohammed Omar, they began what can be described as a reign of terror. It included regular and arbitrary law enforcement by their "Religious Police". For men, this meant severe physical punishments and crimes as ludicrous as insufficient beard length. Gender-based restrictions most notably involved preventing women from free movement and employment, as well as limiting access to education (new rules limited education to Qur'anic studies and until the age of eight).[38] In response to 9/11, the US and its allies launched attacks on Afghanistan which helped to overthrow the Taliban regime. However, since 2005, "the Taliban and other antigovernment forces intensified their insurgency". Taking "advantage of the power vacuum", they "used bombings and assassinations that included attacks on 'soft targets'".[39] The aim, as Human Rights Watch noted, was "to terrorize".[40]

One such assassination involved Shakespeare.

That year, German-Canadian actor and director Corinne Jabber visited Kabul to organise the first Shakespeare play there since the Soviet invasion. She received a clear message: enough blood had been spilt. One actor, Nabi Tanha, explained, "We have lived tragedy for three decades of war. We want to do comedy". Another actor, Shah Mohammed, added that it is "too soon" to perform a tragedy.[41] The director recalls: "I was told from the beginning that they don't want to do tragedy, they don't want to talk about war, they don't want to talk about trauma".[42] The group settled on the comedy Jabber suggested, *Love's Labour's Lost*, eventually performed in the Dari language with the setting moved from the Basque to Afghanistan – specifically, the Bagh-e Babur, or Garden of Babur (Figure 1.3).[43] This UNESCO-protected centuries-old Mughal garden was developed in the early sixteenth century, placing the action in a historical and ancient-feeling setting. The recent battles in the country have left

Figure 1.3 *Love's Labour's Lost* performance in the Babur Garden, Kabul, Afghanistan, 2005 (Tomas Munita/Shutterstock).

bullet marks around the surrounding buildings and walls: a reminder of violence throughout the show. Tanha went on to play Longaville (though initially cast as Berowne) and Mohammed played Ferdinand.

It was a significant fact that women took part in this production. Women had not been allowed to work for six years under the Taliban. One of the leads, teenager Marina Golbahari, had suffered the brunt of the conflict and the education policies: she was largely illiterate and spent her days not in school, but begging around streets and restaurants. Incredibly, after doing so at director Siddiq Barmark's dinner table, she would go on to act in an acclaimed movie, become "probably the best known actress in Afghanistan", and relocate from the refugee camp. After tracking her down for this production, she was cast as Rosaline. Breshna Bahar, a police officer who also acted and was cast as Maria, lost her husband to an artillery round during the civil war.[44] While some of the men would go on to perform on bigger stages (Tanha in *The Kite Runner* and Aref Bahunar, who played Berowne, joined a theatre group in Paris), the consequences were very different for some of their fellow actors, especially the women. Mohammed (Ferdinand) received death threats from the Taliban and is seeking asylum in London.

As for the women, one was thrown out of her family home two weeks before opening night. Saba Sahar – who played the Princess – admitted stresses to her marriage due to her family-in-law's objections. Golbahari received death threats. While travelling with a movie crew, the men in her car were attacked by the Taliban and the equipment destroyed. She sought asylum in Sweden.[45] But for two of the women, the price was even higher. Bahar (who played Maria) was stabbed in the neck by one of her nephews. She survived and is now in France.[46] But the husband of Parwin Mushtahel – cast as an attendant to the Princess –was not as lucky. "I killed my husband with my acting", she says.[47] Initially, Mushtahel and her family were forced to move house due to harassment from neighbours since she was returning from the *Love's Labour's Lost* rehearsals after dark, creating an assumption that she could be a sex worker. Mushtahel was also on the receiving end of death threats from the Taliban during this rehearsal period and would continue to receive threats as her acting profile grew.[48] One day, she was punched to the ground on her way home. Then, after months of receiving calls to tell him to stop his wife from acting, her husband, Tawab, was gunned down outside their home. He left to answer a door but didn't return for hours; Mushtahel heard three gun shots. He was wounded in the face and his body mutilated. She recalls:

> I saw my husband lying down on the floor, his face was full of blood. They didn't allow me to go near his body but you could see that they had shot him so many times.[49]

Mushtahel went into hiding for months before seeking asylum in Canada.

Women have long been used as tools of war and terror – something at the core of Taliban's rule. During the Bosnian War in the 1990s, Serbian forces were notorious not only for ethnic cleansing but also for the mass systemic and genocidal rape of tens of thousands of Bosniak Muslim women. This led to the first recognition and prosecution of mass rape by an international tribunal, whose judges ruled that the tactic was "an instrument of terror".[50] While such an emphasis can risk overshadowing women's roles, such as political activism, in conflict and post-conflict contexts, it has been acknowledged that women bear the brunt of war directly: conflict results in particular issues of gendered violence, displacement, widowhood, and isolation for women.[51] Indeed, "sexual violence, particularly rape, seems part and parcel of most, if not all, conflict", often as an instrument of war. The "total terrorization" of communities and especially women occurs when the motivation for the abuse is the result of an "association between sex and violence", in other words both lust and militarism.[52] The matter extends to domestic violence as "incidents of domestic violence increase during conflict, when militarization becomes the social norm".[53] This abuse could be read into Othello's character and actions towards Desdemona.

In *The Rape of Lucrece*, it is a Roman soldier, Tarquin, who violates Lucrece – all in the context (and middle) of war, with the result of causing yet more war. Even in the mythology of the Trojan War, it is the treatment of women that leads to conflict. In some readings Helen of Troy elopes with Paris but in others she is kidnapped and raped, thus sparking the colossal conflict. Lucrece even compares Tarquin to Paris and responds emotionally to a painting of the Trojan War by noting how "one man's lust these many lives confounds" (1489).

Shakespeare has Tarquin use his tales as a soldier, and in fact those of his comrade, Lucrece's husband Collatine, to entertain her during his visit. Masculinity is linked directly to militarism,[54] a term used to indicate the pervasive "symbols, values, and discourses" that "validate military power".[55] Tarquin uses this gendered notion of militarism as the starting point in his conversation, explaining how Collatine was:

> Made glorious by his manly chivalry
> With bruisèd arms and wreaths of victory.
> (109–10)

The language of battle is clear, even when Tarquin considers Lucrece's immediate beauty. He sees that in her "face Beauty and Virtue strived" (52), making her blush and pale, each state and its features more beautiful than the other. Tarquin sees this beauty in terms of war imagery, culminating in:

> Their silent war of lilies and of roses,
> Which Tarquin viewed in her fair face's field
> (71–72)

He is unable to pick sides, and Tarquin views himself as the third party in this war, deciding to conquer both her beauty and virtue:

> In their pure ranks his traitor eye encloses,
> Where, lest between them both it should be killed,
> The coward captive vanquishèd doth yield
> > To those two armies that would let him go
> > Rather than triumph in so false a foe.
> (73–77)

Though he began by admiring her beauty in a somewhat courtly style, Shakespeare is able to deconstruct disturbingly the poetics of praise to present this soldier's inability to think beyond images of conflict. As such, Tarquin's is also a "military rape" that creates "total terrorization" for Lucrece: it is motivated both by his lust and militarism.

This link is exemplified more craftily elsewhere, like in *The Two Gentlemen of Verona*, when Proteus finds Sylvia alone in the woods and cannot get his way through verbal wooing so warns her about his next course of (violent) action:

Nay, if the gentle spirit of moving words
Can no way change you to a milder form,
I'll woo you like a soldier, at arms' end,
And love you 'gainst the nature of love: force ye.

(5.4.57–60)

Her frightened response – "O heaven!" – is met with confirmation of his intent to switch from verbal to physical harassment: "I'll force thee yield to my desire" (5.4.61–62).

Shakespeare returned to the story of Lucrece several times, most notably in *Titus Andronicus*. Here, Lavinia is raped by Demetrius and Chiron, sons of the Queen of the Goths, as a tool in the battle between them and the Romans. The mutilation of Lavinia's tongue effectively denies her real input in the resolution process. In *Macbeth*, the protagonist's famous dagger soliloquy contemplating his terroristic assassination of King Duncan confirms a parallelism between rape and terror. Macbeth personifies the deed, "withered murder" (2.1.59), that:

With Tarquin's ravishing strides, towards his design
Moves like a ghost.

(2.1.62–63)

Like Tarquin, like every terrorist, Macbeth knows that he has a clear target, as well as the damage he intends to inflict. The "ravishing strides" suggest terror that is not only forceful and destructive but, rather disturbingly, enthralling and satisfying.

Lucrece is mentioned by name by Titus, Marcus, and Aaron in *Titus Andronicus*, Malvolio (twice) in *Twelfth Night*, and Petruchio in *Taming of the Shrew*. Petruchio describes Katherina as Lucrece to indicate her chastity and undermine her. She ends up silenced, as does Lavinia in *Titus Andronicus*. In that play, Lucrece is referenced to highlight Lavinia's chastity and consider whether virtue suggests that she, like Lucrece, should die. Titus settles on a shame killing: "And, with thy shame, thy father's sorrow die!" (5.3.47). Importantly, in Shakespeare's plays, Lucrece – famous for her looks and chastity (as well as the rape and suicide) – is only visualised by male characters.

There have been numerous explorations about the action of naming and its links to power and ownership (for instance, colonisers renaming towns). But *visualising* things in a certain, calculated way is also an effective way of demonstrating power. In the early twentieth century, the French government sent photographers to Algeria create subsidised postcards for the public back home, as documented in *The Colonial Harem*, by Malek Alloula (brother of Abdelkader Alloula). They photographed the architecture and landscape to indicate their possession of the space. When it came to women, they visualised an orientalist image. But they did not find it. Instead, they hired models, often from deprived backgrounds or working in the sex industry, and created studios using props. The results were photographs of Algerian women in harem-like settings, smoking hookahs, in prisons (suggesting captivity), and often topless (suggesting availability). The mystique of the veil and the seduction of the naked body would even be bizarrely combined (Figure 1.4).

The contact of the women's eyes with the lens confirms the enforced nature of the setup. Eye contact is a woman's choice and some choose or have been taught to limit it. During rehearsals of *Love's Labour's Lost*, the "younger women did not look at the men even when they were speaking to them" and despite her efforts, the director "had little success getting them to make eye contact with the men".[56] To add to this, the

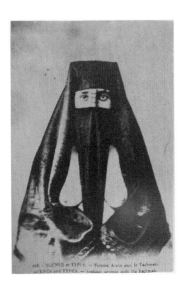

Figure 1.4 Scenes and types: Arabian woman with the Yachmak, 1890s.

power of the Algerian women's dejected glances both speaks to and questions the idealism of the women's eyes in *Love's Labour's Lost* – amidst the disguised dance but most clearly in Berowne's conclusion that the lords' oath should be voided because "love, [is] first learnèd in a lady's eyes" (4.3.329). He even summarises that "From women's eyes this doctrine I derive" (4.3.352). That the women leave the men shortly later indicates a level of delusion on the men's part. Indeed, while the photos in Algeria confirm the power of visualisation, they are essentially illusionary. Like the male characters' references to Lucrece, they show a flawed ideal that the more powerful party is able to maintain, one that is disseminated for an agenda related to perpetuating the power dynamics of gender and conflict. By the 1960s, as a recent exhibition informed, French army officers tasked Marc Garanger with taking photographs of the female FLN prisoners. They removed their headscarves against their will, confirming that "a camera aimed at an unwilling subject is an instrument of torture".[57]

The relevance of this discussion becomes even more striking if linked back to Afghanistan, when the US-led war with the Taliban was often justified in gendered terms – with much visualisation of women wearing the dark face-veil, constantly termed the "burqa", serving effectively as props for the war. The US First Lady at the time, Laura Bush, took over her husband's weekly radio address to make such a point: "Only the terrorists and the Taliban threaten to pull out women's fingernails for wearing nail polish".[58] Writing in *The New Yorker*, Sarah Sentilles dubbed this address an example of how "pseudo-feminism" is "used to justify invasion".[59] Literary theorist Gayatri Spivak has described this kind of rhetoric as "white men are saving brown women from brown men".[60] In 2017, as reported by *The Washington Post*, a national security adviser used a photograph of a woman to convince US President Donald Trump that reducing forces in Afghanistan would be a mistake:

> One of the ways McMaster tried to persuade Trump to recommit to the effort was by convincing him that Afghanistan was not a hopeless place. He presented Trump with a black-and-white snapshot from 1972 of Afghan women in miniskirts walking through Kabul, to show him that Western norms had existed there before and could return.[61]

There is some irony to this specific discussion of dress. Many of the 10,000 Algerian women who joined the FLN's often violent efforts against the French did so by taking off their veils and dressing in "short skirts" so as to access high profile locations to gather intelligence or plant bombs. When this was found out, they reverted to veils. Barbara Harlow notes:

> Whereas it was the veil that had previously taken on a symbolic significance as an assertion of tradition and custom in Algeria, it was Western apparel that early in the revolution allowed Algerian women ... to actively confront the colonial presence. Later, toward the end of the revolution, when Western-clad Algerian women became suspect, the veil was once again assumed by the women of the FLN so that they could conceal within its folds the weapons and explosive devices they carried[.][62]

Although many of these women were charged with terrorist acts, the French regime's own terroristic imprisonment and torture methods are perhaps best represented in the treatment of the women. For example, Djamila Boupacha — a twenty-three-year-old accused of trying to bomb a café — was "illegally imprisoned by French military forces, who subjected her to torture and deflowered her with a bottle".[63] When Marcus sees his niece Lavinia after she is violated in *Titus Andronicus*, he figures the importance of the aftermath, not just the event: "some Tereus hath deflowered thee, / And lest thou shouldst detect him, cut thy tongue" (2.4.26–27). The amnesty of 1962 spared these Algerian women from execution but simultaneously served as their silencer. Practically, the charges of torture Djamila and others had brought against the French army had to be dropped. Rape not only served to terrorise but to shame.

***

Reports note that there were few, if any, women attending the Kabul performance of *Love's Labour's Lost*. The choice of play could be viewed as both relevant and ironic. The premise of the comedy – the King and his lords promising to spend three years refraining from the company of women – has obvious echoes of the restrictions imposed under Taliban rule. The play presents characters traversing social taboos related to love and gender. It appears, then, that by shunning the tragedies, the specific traumas that were being avoided relate to bloodletting on stage, rather than issues that cause thematic discomfort.

On a side note, with the King and his courtiers presented as members of the Afghan royal family (who were actually present on one of the nights) it was not possible for them to disguise as Muscovites. The actors objected: it would be like dressing up as the enemy – insensitive given that ten-year invasion and its lasting impact. Instead, they wear Indian dhotis and dance humorously in Bollywood style. Incidentally, one of the actors, Faisal Azizi, playing Dumaine, wore a T-shirt to hide the shrapnel scars on his arms from a mortar round that hit him and his friends as they sat in the local neighbourhood. He survived but all five of them died instantly.[64]

The premise of *Love's Labour's Lost* is built on the male characters realising, rather inadvertently, that their promise to ignore perceived temptations is specifically like fighting a war, as Ferdinand explains:

> That war against your own affections
> And the huge army of the world's desires –
>
> (1.1.9–10)

This may not be a militaristic war, but through its obvious emphasis on sex, it is still very much a physical one.

The characters agree on a pact, one of:

> strict observances,
> As not to see a woman in that term.
> Which I hope well is not enrollèd there.
> And one day in a week to touch no food,
> And but one meal on every day beside,
> The which I hope is not enrollèd there.
> And then to sleep but three hours in the night,
> And not be seen to wink of all the day –
> When I was wont to think no harm all night
> And make a dark night too of half the day –
> The which I hope is not enrollèd there.
> O, these are barren tasks, too hard to keep:
> Not to see ladies, study, fast, not sleep.
>
> (1.1.36–48)

Ironically, these men use their own privileged position of freedom to embark on a restricted existence of "strict observances" that, for most Afghanis, was enforced by the Taliban – most obviously public relationships between men and women, coupled with an invisibility based on dress codes and lack of access to public life that means they will not "see a woman" or "see ladies". In fact, in 2011, Western media repeated the title "Afghanistan's *Romeo and Juliet*" when the Taliban planned to sentence two teenagers to death for pre-marital sex.[65] In the Afghani context, the oaths in the play become less of an unassuming springboard for comic exploration of the human condition and instead appear negative and barely light-hearted. Through the very first speech of the play, the lords are the unbeknown terrorisers – ironically, of themselves.

The imminent arrival of the Princess and her ladies inevitably shatters the oath and its restrictions. It is only through the visible presence and active influence of the women that the oppression can be challenged. In fact, that the play ends on an ambiguous note shows the need for ongoing efforts to bring about peace and equality: there is no magic, comic solution. Yes, in ceasing to believe in their ascetic ideals and in expressing their love openly without disguise, the men may have moved from a Taliban-like state to a post-Taliban state. As Sahar put it, the Taliban era and the play both show that "people will force their way past the limitations".[66] But the women leave abruptly and set conditions for the men – ones which do not involve unrealistic and self-absorbed fasting but the simple demand of pragmatic, self-preserving loyalty. By dictating this ending, and indeed controlling the future events post-play, it is the women who hold the key to the resolution of conflict in this plot and beyond it. Here is a conclusion in which there is no real conclusion – and it is up to the women, not the men, whether there will be a *Love's Labour's Won*.

On a somewhat optimistic level, the play could be seen as an opportunity to appreciate the very existence of love. As expressed by Azizi, the Taliban would "never allow us to put on a play, to tell a story about love. Now we have a democracy and we can show these things to our people".[67] More pragmatically, as Sahar relates:

Love is not new in this country. . . . But you can't tell people, oh, I've fallen in love. There's lots of change from that black period until now, the Taliban period, when you couldn't even walk with your own husband in the street. In this time, we

have lots of freedom. But love is still something you should
keep secret.[68]

Love's Labour's Lost, then, is most suitable in that it complicates
that simple sentiment of love. It also explains what the
secrecy of love can affect: the King and the lords keep their
love for the respective ladies secret from one another and the
end product is not exactly positive; not quite as fatal as the
consequences for the secret love of Romeo and Juliet, but
also without the resolution of the other comedies. Societal
restrictions on love are real: I recall a noticeable number of
love messages etched on the beautiful mountains overlooking
the Yemeni city of Ibb, most of them lamenting a loved one
about to be married to another man or complaining that
the couple can't marry due to societal restrictions (real-life
Romeos and Juliets). Given the situation in Yemen today, one
can't help but be reminded of slogans about making love not
war. Of course, it's not that simple, but the social taboos, like
that oath, really can be the invisible terroriser. To give a contrary example, despite issues surrounding Prospero's control,
the world of *The Tempest* is far from secretive about Ferdinand
and Miranda's future together: their marriage is therefore
never in any real doubt.

The key struggle presented by *Love's Labour's Lost* involves
meditation and study on one hand, with love and lovemaking on the other. But what the play does not do is deny
the existence of love. The characters, like the audience, like the
oppressors, know that love must exist. As such, the creation
of doctrine and taboos cannot curtail love, but lovemaking.
By the end, the characters have experienced frustrations on
both fronts: what they chose not to have (love) and what they
cannot have (lovemaking). The title makes more sense than

ever: the labours of love are lost and the play is about how we might possibly regather them.

The play's verbally complicated messaging has often been linked to Armado's letter, which Ferdinand reads aloud in the first scene, italicised in the original quarto:

But to the place, where? It standeth north-north-east and by east from the west corner of thy curious-knotted garden;

(1.1.225–27)

The "curious-knotted" Elizabethan garden design – suggesting symmetrical formality as well as elaborate variation – has been regarded as a summary of the play's rhetorical complexities. But it is also a demonstration of the way in which love transpires: a mixture of arrangement and ornament. Either, the process of finding love is itself the key to love, which is the final decoration. Just as a rom-com doesn't work without a struggle, it is the chase and anticipation that we cherish. Or, taking it further, arrangement represents love and ornament is the consummation.

This garden imagery is even more significant when we remember that the Kabul production culminated at the Garden of Babur. With only a tent and carpet as scenery, the crumbling historical garden became both setting and set, complete with the rocket and bullet damage riddled around it. UNESCO categorises the location as an "Islamic garden", which it defines as follows:

The old-Iranian word for such gardens *"pari-daizi"* expresses the notion of an earthly paradise which is inherent to them … Islamic gardens are multi-functional: they not only serve contemplation and relaxation, but are also a

representation and manifestation of power ... [H]olding
audiences and celebrating victories or marriages in these
gardens signal superiority, or social and political bonds.[69]

This garden offers an alternative but similarly paradoxical
symbolism for the play and its theme of love. As an earthly
paradise, the setting is a reminder of how this chase of love can
be both a divine action and a fall from grace. Such a garden's
role emphasises both "relaxation" and "power"; it is a space
to celebrate "victories or marriages". In this setting, the links
between love and marriage on one hand and social and political contexts on the other becomes clearer. Both are types
of authority. Of course, the play has been read as exploring
the early modern humanistic approach: a rationalist system
of thought attaching prime importance to human knowledge
rather than divine or supernatural matters. But in this setting,
what seems like a simple desire (love) is complicated because
of the difficulty of manifesting that desire into a reality (lovemaking). This confirmed complication is at the heart of *Love's
Labour's Lost*, a play that offers, at once, a simple yet complex plot.

EPILOGUE: "THE KING LIKE NOT THE COMEDY"

The consequences of clumping Shakespeare with the West
have been made visible in Shakespeare-related terror attacks
in Qatar and Afghanistan. But the history of perceiving
Shakespeare as Western can't be restricted solely as a terroristic concern. Broadly speaking, in many parts of the world,
responses to Shakespeare have in one way or another been
direct or indirect responses to issues of colonisation and
external influence.

The tragedy of comedy

As the French photographs of the Algerian women demonstrate, the colonial mission extended well beyond control of the economy and education. Harlow highlights the photographs as an attempt to penetrate "the secret, tantalizing recesses of the harem" in much the same way as some European travellers embarked on "masqueraded pilgrimage to Mecca".[70] These include the Victorian "traveller" Richard Francis Burton, whose mid-nineteenth-century trip to Mecca is well documented. On his travels, Burton carried his copy of Shakespeare's works, probably a pocket version, which he would read "again and again".[71] When it comes to cultural imperialism, how much has really changed? A century and a half later, Dominic Dromgoole's world tour of *Hamlet* implied the global presence of Shakespeare but received much criticism for its approach of taking a British Shakespeare out to the world; one reviewer named it "neo-colonialism". That they didn't perform in Syria and North Korea is worth mention: governments perceived in the West to engage in state-sponsored terror but whose own narrative is that the West sponsors dissident terrorism against them. Those countries don't deserve Shakespeare, apparently, but maybe they don't want it. Cultural imperialism can be perceived as a threat and in these contexts Shakespeare can be interpreted as a dangerous tool representing colonial history, external infiltration, and foreign policy.

There is some evidence of this, too. *Henry V* has been used in military contexts for decades as a way of boosting morale and inspiration. The Armed Services Editions given to British soldiers in World War Two included a pocketbook of *Henry V*. Its most famous scene, just as the English are about to attack the French port of Harfleur, sees Henry urging his soldiers to fire themselves up for battle:

Once more unto the breach, dear friends, once more,
Or close the wall up with our English dead.
In peace there's nothing so becomes a man
As modest stillness and humility,
But when the blast of war blows in our ears,
Then imitate the action of the tiger:
Stiffen the sinews, summon up the blood,
Disguise fair nature with hard-favoured rage,
Then lend the eye a terrible aspect:
Let it pry through the portage of the head
Like the brass cannon,

(3.1.1–11)

Henry is unequivocal in his message: kill or be killed. And what follows is a serious amount of bloodshed.

More recently, the play has continued to be utilised in military; free copies of Henry V were distributed to US troops serving in Afghanistan and Iraq.[72]

Responses to Shakespeare also confirm the gendered nature of terrorism. In the discussed cases, there exists a clearly patriarchal structure to conflict – almost always the violence is from men. But Mushtahel, who acted in Love's Labour's Lost, is still alive; her husband, who never acted, was cruelly assassinated. The Taliban punished the man. A ministerial document distributed to the Taliban's law enforcers includes numerous such examples:

1 To prevent sedition and uncovered females (be hejab): No drivers are allowed to pick up females who are using Iranian burqa. In the case of violation the driver will be imprisoned. If such kinds of female are observed in the street, their houses will be found and *their husbands punished*.

9 To prevent washing clothes by young ladies along the
   water streams in the city: It should be announced in all
   mosques and the matter should be monitored. Violator
   ladies should be picked up with respectful Islamic
   manner, taken to their houses and *their husbands
   severely punished*.

13 To prevent music and dances in wedding parties: To be
   broadcasted by the public information resources that
   the above two things should be prevented. In the case
   of violation *the head of the family will be arrested and
   punished*.

15 To prevent sewing ladies' cloth and taking female body
   measures by tailors: If women or fashion magazines are
   seen in the shop *the tailor should be imprisoned*.[73]

The difficulties and consequences the women face as a result
of this tactic become exacerbated: the violence to the man
becomes an act of terror towards both the man *and* woman.
What is more, by bringing women into the conflict, the
stakes are raised for the men to control the women, making it
even more difficult for women and further perpetuating the
patriarchy.

When it comes to clothing, a pattern emerges. In Egypt,
during the *sahwah*, women's dress represented a combination
of religious zeal and anti-colonial sentiment. During the revolution in Iran, women collectively reassumed the veil, again
symbolic. In Algeria, the veil was limited, but women wore it
symbolically, then practically as disguise to help their resistance. In Afghanistan, some women wore the veil to hold onto
their identity. These actions show the importance of freedom
in a resistance narrative; we hate what we are forced to adopt
or scrap. A particularly pertinent example is mentioned by

Kenyan writer Ngugi wa Thiong'o, who describes how the British effort against female circumcision was met with an increase as Kenyan women demanded their right to a national and gendered identity through the very act of circumcision.

Shakespeare is not oblivious to such gendered conversations. In *All's Well That Ends Well*, Bertram finds an excuse for abandoning his bride by joining in a war in Italy as a mercenary, confirming and exploiting the constant link between masculinity and conflict. In Shakespeare's time, clothing was a stated aspect of politics: Elizabeth I's *Proclamation against Excess of Apparel* (1574) regulated, through sumptuary laws, the fabrics and colours that each social class could wear. This served to stratify society and to limit extravagant spending that could damage the local economy, especially as the luxurious fabrics were imported. This is all very close to Shakespeare: in the Induction to *The Taming of the Shrew*, the drunkard Christopher Sly begins to believe he is a Lord when he is dressed in expensive clothing. In private theatres, elitist audience members would sit on the edges of the stage itself to show off their fashionable attires. With cross dressing and the emergence of public theatre, though, the plays disrupt these regulations.

Shakespeare uses clothing to advance his plot when men wear women's clothes, like in *The Merry Wives of Windsor*, and women disguise as men in *As You Like It, Cymbeline, The Merchant of Venice*, and *Twelfth Night*. In *Henry IV, Part Two*, the soldier Ancient Pistol violently tears prostitute Doll Tearsheet's ruff off her body, at once stripping her of the right to aspire for higher social status and reinforcing the patriarchal setup that sees men controlling when she undresses. But it is in *The Taming of the Shrew* that Shakespeare shows the vital symbolism of women's clothing. Indeed, the play is a response to the law against "scolds" or "shrews"; Katherina, remember, is "Renowned in Padua for her scolding tongue" (1.2.92). This crime was not removed from English law until 1967, incidentally the year of Franco Zeffirelli's *Taming of the Shrew* movie starring Elizabeth Taylor. Those convicted were punished through a form of forced attire: the scold's brank or bridle. The iron muzzle, like a mask, was placed on the woman's face and included a metal plate that forces the tongue down so she cannot speak as she is paraded publicly. In *Taming*, Katherina is not allowed to wear the dress she has had designed for Bianca's wedding despite loving it: "I never saw a better-fashioned gown, / More quaint, more pleasing, nor more commendable" (4.1.104–05). When she tries to wear the hat, since "gentlewomen wear such caps as these", Petruchio confirms control through clothing: "When you are gentle, you shall have one too" (4.1.72–73). Petruchio undermines Katherina by forcing her to wear simple clothes that do not conform to her status or, importantly, her sense of self. It is the story of any woman forced to wear or remove clothing and confirms hierarchies of power and perceived civilisation. For Petruchio, the clothing symbolises control. For Katherina, it symbolises freedom of expression: "I will be free / Even to the uttermost, as I please, in words" (4.3.82–83) – and freedom of choice: "Love me or love me not, I like the cap, / And it I will have, or I will have none" (4.3.87–88). In the play, clothing plays a similar role to the universal rights of food and sleep. Shakespeare confirms and complicates clothing as a palpable, gendered battleground.

The reception linking to terror is specifically useful in challenging one particular aspect about Shakespeare's canon: the assumed superiority of tragedy. Which plays caused havoc?

Midsummer Night's Dream (Iran), *Twelfth Night* (Qatar), *Taming of the Shrew* (Algeria), *Love's Labour's Lost* (Afghanistan). In short, it is Shakespearean comedy that is most problematic to terrorists.

On the face of it, tragedy appears more serious, clearer in its messaging of good versus evil; any symbolic comment on authority is easier to spot. But comedy seems to have hidden meanings. The harder it is to put your finger on it, the more feared it is, the more it exacerbates paranoia. The authoritarian or fanatic is left to wonder: "Hum! Conspiracy?" (*King Lear* 1.2.50).[74]

When Abdelkader Alloula – who had performed in *Taming* – was assassinated in 1990s Algeria, he was working on an Arabic production of Molière's *Tartuffe*, a comedy that has upset authority since its first performance (and suppression) in 1664. As a director and writer, Alloula publicly advocated humour on the stage above didacticism, describing comedy as the best way to observe and advance society. Comic theatre comes to represent a form of expression. However, the terrorising response is not necessarily because of the content of the expression, but rather, the mere existence of free expression. To put it another way, at what point does the terror happen? In the example from Iran, the thugs were placed in the audience before the play even started, and in Afghanistan, some actors suffered even before the opening night. Artistic expression is convoluted with and within freedom of expression.

Kabir Rahimi, who played the Messengers in the Kabul *Love's Labour's Lost*, reflected that:

> By listening to Shakespeare, those with guilty consciences suffer. ... By doing this play, we will bring our suffering to

those with guilty consciences who are still in this country and ruling us. That is why we must invite them, the warlords.[75]

But the anti-terroristic Shakespeare is only one side of the story. The other side of the story is that the terrorists who attacked Shakespeare have also missed the point. And Bin Laden, like many teenagers, probably wasn't paying attention. Shakespeare knew about terrorism and his plays and characters explore the terrorist mindset.

Shakespearean comedy will simply continue to be performed regardless:

> For if the king like not the comedy,
> Why then, belike, he likes it not
> > (*Hamlet* 3.2.254–55)

Shakespearean tragedy? It has inspired terrorists.

NOTES

1 Azadeh Ganjeh, "Performing *Hamlet* in Modern Iran (1900–2012)", PhD diss. (Bern University, 2017), 12.
2 S. Habib Mousavi and Babak Rajabi, "The Bard Goes to the East: Shakespeare in Iran", in *Culture-Blind Shakespeare: Multiculturalism and Diversity*, ed. Maryam Beyad and Ali Salami (Newcastle upon Tyne: Cambridge Scholars, 2016), 125.
3 In fact, the BBC has long been linked to interference in Iranian politics. Mohammad Reza Pahlavi accused BBC Farsi Radio of helping to instigate the revolution of 1979. The station also aired all of Ayatollah Khomeini's public speeches and analysed them favourably. And during the 2009 protests, Ayatollah Khamenei accused BBC Farsi TV of instigating demonstrations.
4 Mahmood Karimi-Hakak, in conversation with Islam Issa (February 2021), unless otherwise stated.

5   Mahmood Karimi-Hakak, "Exiled to Freedom: A Memoir of Censorship in Iran", TDR/The Drama Review 47.4 (2003): 17–50, 25.

6   Ibid., 32.

7   Peter C. Herman, "Equity and the Problem of Theseus in A Midsummer Night's Dream: Or, the Ancient Constitution in Ancient Athens", Journal for Early Modern Cultural Studies 14.1 (Winter 2014): 4–31.

8   The Last Imam is Muhammad al-Mahdi, an eschatological messianic figure whom the majority of Shi'ites believe to be alive in occultation until he returns to bring redemptive justice.

9   Karimi-Hakak, "Exiled to Freedom", 38–40.

10 Demonstrating this fascinating power dynamic, on one occasion, the broadcast of a Khamenei statement due to air live at the usual slot after the 9 p.m. news was delayed for twenty-four hours so that Grigori Kozintsev's 1964 Hamlet movie could conclude. See Kazem Vahdat, "When Hamlet's Film Prevents the Broadcast of the Iranian Leader's Statement", Kazem Vahdat Blog (no date), http://kazemvahdat.blog.ir/post/leader-speech [accessed 11 February 2021].

11 These terms were used in the context of media reception by cultural theorist Stuart Hall; see his "Encoding and Decoding in the Media Discourse", Stencilled Paper 7 (1973): 90–103.

12 Ika Willis, Reception (New York: Routledge, 2018), 95. The term "disidentification" has been used by José Esteban Muñoz. "Famous and Dandy Like B. 'N' Andy: Race, Pop and Basquiat", in Pop Out: Queer Warhol ed. Jennifer Doyle, Jonathan Flatley, and José Esteban Muñoz (Durham: Duke University Press, 1996), 152–53.

13 Oriana Fallaci, "An Interview with KHOMEINI", New York Times (7 October 1979), 8.

14 I do not use the word fatwa in this context because it is an important term referring to an authoritative legal opinion given by a legal scholar, but has been overused in this context to the extent that it can now denote controversial opinions and the issuance of death penalties.

15 For a critical-creative account of this event based on some primary research, see Graham Holderness, Tales from Shakespeare: Creative Collisions (Cambridge: Cambridge University Press, 2014), 207–25.

16 "Protest Rally over Qatar Bombing", BBC News (21 March 2015), http://news.bbc.co.uk/2/hi/middle_east/4368267.stm [accessed 1 November 2019]; Alwasat, "Hujūm al-doḥa nafadhahu miṣriy

bi-sayyāratih al-khāṣṣah", www.alwasatnews.com/news/454270.html [accessed 1 November 2019]; Al Jazeera, "Maqtal brīṭānī fī infijār sayārah mufakhakhah fī qaṭar", www.aljazeera.net/ news/ arabic/ 2005/ 3/ 20/ مقتل-بريطاني-في-انفجار-سيارة-مفخخة-بقطر [accessed 1 November 2019].

17 For instance, a request to visit or interview for my BBC Radio 3 documentary was kindly declined as the group felt they did not want to keep recalling the trauma.

18 Islam Issa, *Milton in the Arab-Muslim World* (New York: Routledge, 2016), 44.

19 For summaries of these contexts, see ibid., 43–46, 53–54.

20 Asafa Jalata, *Phases of Terrorism in the Age of Globalization: From Christopher Columbus to Osama bin Laden* (New York: Palgrave Macmillan, 2016), 92–93.

21 Algerian Embassy in London, "The National Anthem", www.algerianembassy.org.uk/index.php/national-anthem.html [accessed 29 October 2019].

22 Thousands of Arabs joined the Afghan-Soviet War (1979–89). It was both legal and regarded widely as a religious duty. It is thought that the fighters were supported by Saudi Arabia and even the CIA in order to defeat the Russians. When they returned to their countries, though some were arrested, they were generally regarded as heroes. Among the thousands were Bin Laden and Ayman al-Zawahiri. The Palestinian Abdullah Azzam, Bin Laden's mentor, was one of the key popularisers of the movement before going on to co-found al-Qaeda. In 1989, Azzam was assassinated (theories about who carried this out vary, including the CIA, Iran, Mossad, and al-Qaeda themselves).

23 The most striking account is by former special forces officer Habib Souaidïa in his book *La sale guerre: Le témoignage d'un ancien officier des forces de l'armée algérienne* [The Dirty War: The Testimony of a Former Officer of the Algerian Armed Forces] (Paris: Éditions La Découverte, 2001), which also claims that Islamist attacks were supported by the government, or "invisible powers", to justify their own cause. It has also been claimed that prominent SIF members were governmental secret agents.

24 John Esposito, *Unholy War: Terror in the Name of Islam* (Oxford: Oxford University Press, 2002), 61.

25 John Esposito, *The Islamic Threat: Myth or Reality* (Oxford: Oxford University Press, 1999), 138.

26 John Esposito, *The Oxford Dictionary of Islam* (Oxford: Oxford University Press, 2003), 154.

27 Esposito, *The Islamic Threat*, 138.

28 Gilles Kepel, *Jihad: The Trail of Political Islam* (Cambridge, MA: Harvard University Press, 2002), 31.

29 Jassim Muhalhal al-Yassin, "Ḥadīth al-Usbūʿ: Sayyid Quṭb" [Dialogue of the Week: Sayyid Qutb], *al-Watan* (4 March 2008).

30 On *al-Risālah* magazine, see Issa, Milton in the *Arab-Muslim World*, 53.

31 Sayyid Qutb, "Al-tarjamah wa nahḍat Miṣr al-thaqāfiyyah" [Translation and Egypt's Cultural Renaissance], *al-Risālah* 617 (7 May 1945).

32 Sayyid Qutb, "ʿAlā hāmish al-naqd: al-rābiṭ al-muqaddas" [On the Margins of Criticism: The Sacred Bond], *al-Risālah* 598 (18 December 1944).

33 Sayyid Qutb, "ʿAlā hāmish al-naqd: Shylok al-jadeed aw qaḍiyyat Filisṭīn" [On the Margins of Criticism: The New Shylock or the Case of Palestine], *al-Risālah* 655 (21 January 1946). Bakathir, an Indonesian originally from Yemen, was a successful playwright in Egypt.

34 Sayyid Qutb, "The America I Have Seen" (1951), in *America in an Arab Mirror: Images of America in Arabic Travel Literature, 1668 to 9/11 and Beyond*, ed. Kamal Abdel-Malek and Mouna El Kahla (New York: Palgrave Macmillan, 2011), 9–27, 26.

35 Suggestions that Qutb's literary criticism should be separated from his political ideology because of when they were written do not stand since his writings about the US, which were *before* his literary criticism, are often cited as proof of his views and their formation. John C. Zimmerman, "Sayyid Qutb's Influence on the 11 September Attacks", *Terrorism and Political Violence* 16.2 (2004): 22–252, 223 notes:

> Qutb's writings can be divided into three broad chronological time frames. His first phase began in the 1930s as a literary critic. The second phase began in the late 1940s and lasted until 1964 when he devoted his writings to the necessity of establishing a society following strict Islamic adherence. Although imprisoned from 1954–64, he continued his writings from a jail cell. The third phase began in 1964 when

he added to his Islamic writings the need to overthrow all existing governments by force if necessary.

36 Qutb, "The America I Have Seen", 24.

37 Muhammad Ismail and Ahmed Arafa, "Istmirār ʻfitnat Sayyid Quṭb dākhil al-ikhwān", Youm 7, https://www.youm7.com/story/2015/5/4/ 2167933 /استمرار-فتنة-سيد-قطب-داخل-الإخوان-القرضاوى-يواصل-حملته-قطب [accessed 9 November 2019].

38 Physicians for Human Rights, The Taliban's War on Women: A Health and Human Rights Crisis in Afghanistan (Boston: Physicians for Human Rights, 1998), 2–4.

39 Rosemarie Skaine, Women of Afghanistan in the Post-Taliban Era: How Lives Have Changed and Where They Stand Today (London: McFarland, 2008), 10.

40 Human Rights Watch, "Afghanistan: Events of 2006", World Report 2007.

41 Qais Akbar Omar and Stephen Landrigan, A Night in the Emperor's Garden: A True Story of Hope and Resilience in Afghanistan (London: Haus, 2015), 47.

42 Shakespeare from Kabul, directed by Harriet Shawcross (Scott White Pictures, 2012).

43 The first four performances were at a different location and hundreds of people attended. For a detailed account of this performance, see Omar and Landrigan, A Night in the Emperor's Garden. For an account and analysis of this performance, including interviews with the director, see William C. Carroll, "Love's Labour's Lost in Afghanistan", Shakespeare Bulletin 28.4 (2010): 443–58.

44 Omar and Landrigan, A Night in the Emperor's Garden, 69, 71–77, 89–90.

45 Ibid., 229, 246; Stephen Landrigan, "Where There's a Will", The Guardian "Shortcuts" (8 September 2005), www.theguardian.com/theguardian/ 2005/sep/08/features11.g2 [accessed 9 November 2019].

46 Omar and Landrigan, A Night in the Emperor's Garden, 241.

47 Tom Coghlan, "Paween Mushtakhel Is Forced into Hiding as Taleban Return to Kabul", The Times (2 March 2009).

48 Omar and Landrigan, A Night in the Emperor's Garden, 128–29.

49 BBC News, "Terrifying Plight of Afghan Actress" (25 March 2009), http://news.bbc.co.uk/2/hi/south_asia/7940527.stm [accessed 9 November 2019]; Omar and Landrigan, A Night in the Emperor's Garden, 231–32.

50 Olivera Simic, *Regulation of Sexual Conduct in UN Peacekeeping Operations* (Heidelberg: Springer, 2012), 65.

51 Meredith Turshen, "Women's War Stories", in *What Women Do in Wartime*, ed. Meredith Turshen and Clotilde Twagiramariya (London: Zed Books, 1998), 1–26.

52 Ibid., 12. "Total terrorization" is a phrase used by Roland Littlewood, "Military Rape", *Anthropology Today* 13.2 (1997): 7–16, 13.

53 Joyce P. Kaufman and Kristen P. Williams, *Women and War: Gender Identity and Activism in Times of Conflict* (Sterling: Kumarian Press, 2010), 10, 36.

54 Turshen, "Women's War Stories", 5.

55 Robin Luckham, "The Military, Militarization and Democratization in Africa: A Survey of Literature and Issues", *African Studies Review* 37.2 (1994): 13–75, 24.

56 Omar and Landrigan, *A Night in the Emperor's Garden*, 84.

57 Rian Dundon, "These Algerian Women Were Forced to Remove Their Veils to Be Photographed in 1960", *Timeline* (20 December 2016), https://timeline.com/photos-women-french-algeria-98ee46628854 [accessed 9 November 2019].

58 "Text: Laura Bush on Taliban Oppression of Women", *Washington Post* (17 November 2001), www.washingtonpost.com/wp-srv/nation/specials/attacked/transcripts/laurabushtext_111701.html [accessed 9 November 2019].

59 Sarah Sentilles, "Colonial Postcards and Women as Props for War-Making", *New Yorker* (5 October 2017), www.newyorker.com/books/second-read/colonial-postcards-and-women-as-props-for-war-making [accessed 9 November 2019].

60 G. C. Spivak, "Can the Subaltern Speak?", in *Colonial Discourse and Postcolonial Theory: A Reader*, ed. Patrick Williams Laura Chrisman (Hemel Hempstead: Harvester, 1993), 93.

61 Philip Rucker and Robert Costa, "'It's a Hard Problem': Inside Trump's Decision to Send More Troops to Afghanistan", *Washington Post* (21 August 2017), www.washingtonpost.com/politics/its-a-hard-problem-inside-trumps-decision-to-send-more-troops-to-afghanistan/2017/08/21/14dcb126-868b-11e7-a94f-3139abce39f5_story.html [accessed 9 November 2019].

62 Barbara Harlow, "Introduction", in Malek Alloula, *The Colonial* Harem, trans. Myrna Godzich and Wlad Godzich (Minneapolis: University of Minnesota Press, 1986), ix–xxii, x.

63 Simone de Beauvoir and Gisèle Halimi, *Djamila Boupacha: The Story of the Torture of a Young Algerian Girl Which Shocked Liberal French Opinion*, trans. Peter Green (London: Andre Deutsch and Weidenfeld & Nicholson, 1962), 9.

64 Omar and Landrigan, *A Night in the Emperor's Garden*, 53, 169.

65 Ted Thornhill, "Afghanistan's Romeo and Juliet: Teenage Couple Jailed and Face Being Stoned for Falling in Love", *Daily Mail* (1 August 2011), www.dailymail.co.uk/news/article-2021147/Teenage-couple-jailed-face-execution-falling-love.html [accessed 21 January 2021].

66 Omar and Landrigan, *A Night in the Emperor's Garden*, 106.

67 Tom Coghlan, "Bard Makes Kabul Comeback after 27 Years", *Telegraph* (7 September 2005), www.telegraph.co.uk/news/worldnews/asia/afghanistan/1497846/Bard-makes-Kabul-comeback-after-27-years.html [accessed 9 November 2019].

68 Scott Baldauf, "Love's 'Labour' Not a Lost Cause in Kabul", *Christian Science Monitor* (1 September 2005), www.csmonitor.com/2005/0901/p07s01-wosc.html [accessed 9 November 2019].

69 UNESCO, "Bagh-e Babur", *UNESCO World Heritage Centre* https://whc.unesco.org/en/tentativelists/5469/ [accessed 6 November 2019].

70 Harlow, "Introduction", xvi.

71 Richard Francis Burton, *Zanzibar: City, Island and Coast*, vol. 2 (1872), 388–89. For more on Burton's Shakespeare, see Edward Wilson-Lee, *Shakespeare in Swahililand: In Search of a Global Poet* (London: William Collins, 2016).

72 Diana E. Henderson, "Meditations in a Time of (Displaced) War: Henry V, Money, and the Ethics of Performing History", in *Shakespeare and War*, ed. Ros King and Paul J. C. M. Franssen (Basingstoke: Palgrave Macmillan, 2008), 226–27. See also the introduction to Adam McKeown, *English Mercuries: Soldier Poets in the Age of Shakespeare* (Nashville: Vanderbilt University Press, 2009), in which he reflects on teaching Henry V to fellow US troops in Djibouti.

73 "Appendix C", Physicians for Human Rights, *The Taliban's War on Women: A Health and Human Rights Crisis in Afghanistan* (Boston: Physicians for Human Rights, 1998), 117–19; emphasis mine.

74 The edition being used, which follows the First Folio but is informed by the quartos, has two exclamation points. The First Folio print has two question marks. I have therefore settled on my own interpretation of this phrase as exclamation followed by question.

75 Omar and Landrigan, *A Night in the Emperor's Garden*, 102–3.

Freedom and principled violence

Two

FREEDOM AND DEATH

Robben Island's maximum security jail held political prisoners during South Africa's institutional apartheid (1948–1994). Confined to religious texts, the prisoners sneaked Shakespeare's *Complete Works* as a sacred Hindu text. As the edition was passed around, inmates made a deal to annotate the passages that spoke to them most. On 16 December 1979, one of them, a revolutionary by the name of Nelson Mandela, signed his name next to a speech by Julius Caesar:

> Cowards die many times before their deaths,
> The valiant never taste of death but once.
> Of all the wonders that I yet have heard,
> It seems to me most strange that men should fear,
> Seeing that death, a necessary end,
> Will come when it will come.
>
> *(Julius Caesar* 2.2.33–38)

On one level, it is inspiring that these words spoke to a man who was seventeen years into his life sentence and could be led to his execution at any moment.

The act of reading and interpreting is itself a type of freedom. As recently as the nineteenth century, anti-literacy

DOI: 10.4324/9780429320088-3

laws in the US prohibited "blacks" from learning how to read or write, with severe punishments that included floggings for "whites" who taught them. Slaves were banned from reading for a reason: education is a route to freedom.

In the case of this Robben Island Shakespeare, the symbolic freedom to read is sought in response to – and perhaps in conjunction with – the limitation of actual, physical freedom. We will never know the extent to which exposure to Shakespeare altered Mandela's views about death in that moment. But as the critic Ewan Fernie notes, far from confirming some sort of Shakespearean universality, the Robben Island edition highlights how prisoners had to bear an

> urgently specific truth, that you've got to find the courage
> to die, even if that means to die violently, a truth which
> Mandela apparently found in Shakespeare, and one which
> may very well have stiffened his resolve[.][1]

The notion of prisoners identifying with death as one of their realities is striking. Adding to the link between symbolic and physical freedoms, it constructs a further link between these freedoms and death itself. In other words, the perception of freedom can also encompass, to use Fernie's phrase, "the courage to die". And it certainly does for one key Shakespearean character who tries to discover his conception of freedom by questioning, directly, whether to live or die. This is, of course, Hamlet.

As the previous chapter concluded, Shakespeare's comedies appear to have been problematic to terrorists in different contexts. As we shall see, tragedies are more likely to inspire them. Before looking at such examples, though, this chapter proposes that it is specifically Shakespeare's *characters* who can inspire terrorists. To commence this line of argument, I first reconsider aspects of Hamlet's context and character in the play, both atmospherically and through textual analysis.

Don John in *Much Ado About Nothing*, Iago in *Othello*, Richard in *Richard III*, Aaron in *Titus Andronicus*: it is assumed knowledge that these characters are villains and criminals. The traits they have in common, and their unapologetic, almost stoic attitudes, help us to identify them as antagonists. What is more, they each attack a series of common values, like matrimonial love. They are the terrorising aggressors of whom we are effortlessly aware, who waste no time telling us as much and whose early soliloquies are utilised to confirm the aggression. In the first scene of *Richard III*, he declares: "I am determinèd to prove a villain" (1.1.30). In the first scene of *Othello*, Iago ends a speech by stating: "I am not what I am" (1.1.67). Not a difficult or remote phrase: six monosyllabic words, and easy enough for a child to understand. Iago is saying, most simply, that he is pretending to be Othello's friend and confidant, whereas he really isn't. But imagine for a moment that you've ended a nice lunch outing with your best friend who then looks you straight in the eye and says, "I am not what I am". It's chilling: much more powerful a phrase than might first appear, and with implications beyond the mere plot. In a defining moment of Exodus, "God said unto Moses: I AM THAT I AM" (3.14). In Hebrew, "'*ehyeh 'asher 'ehyeh*" – the first person "I am" is *'ehyeh*; the third person "he is" would be *yahweh*, later mis-transcribed as Jehovah. Iago's declaration of "I am not what I am", then, is in direct contrast to the Abrahamic God's self-revelation to Moses at the burning bush, now taken as "I am what I am". Iago is not simply in opposition to Othello, but to human instinct, to the cosmos, and ultimately, to God. On top of that, any actor standing on a stage who says "I am not what I am" is certainly not lying.[2]

Hamlet's soliloquies, though, serve a different and by most accounts more complicated purpose than confirming or self-proclaiming villainy. Hamlet's contemplative nature makes his eventual violence appear more principled. His legacy makes him a much admired character — and that is certainly valid. But it is far from the complete picture. This chapter introduces a reading of terror within the dramatic world of an exemplary play. By building on the thorough, policy-informing research of leading criminologist Imran Awan into the terrorist mentality, I propose that we can reread aspects of Hamlet's character — both more sympathetically and more sinisterly. Here, we return the introduction's findings about the terrorist formation. Terrorists are most often:

- seeking actual or symbolic freedom;
- carrying (often unaddressed) trauma;
- contemplative, rational actors;
- inspired by ideology;
- concerned with symbolism;
- ultimately violent.

HAMLET: TERRORIST OR FREEDOM FIGHTER?

SEEKING ACTUAL OR SYMBOLIC FREEDOM. CARRYING (OFTEN UNADDRESSED) TRAUMA. CONTEMPLATIVE, RATIONAL ACTORS

Describing his life, Hamlet says that "Denmark's a prison" (2.2.239). He isn't lying. Kronborg Castle, where Shakespeare imagined Hamlet's home, has no escape. When I made my way to visit the Renaissance castle built in 1585, the first thing I noticed was the series of moats and gates separating the town of Helsingør (Elsinore in the play) from the castle's outskirts. After some uphill walking, one feels the castle's presence at the extreme northeastern tip of Denmark's Zealand island, on a high foreland that has a sheer, vertical drop straight into the sea. The foreland overhangs, almost floats, into the narrowest point of the Sound (Øresund, the strait between Denmark and Sweden) as if it is neither here nor there. The sky is clear and panoramic from the courtyards. From Helsingør, the ferry takes a very short time to get to Helsingborg in Sweden, just two and a half miles away.

Hamlet could only see the deadly sea below him, the endless sky above him, the confining fortifications behind him, and unreachable Sweden in front of him – so close that it almost feels graspable, yet still too far away. And by the time I left, it was so foggy that I could no longer even see the other side of the water (Figure 2.1).

Hamlet is a young man who wants freedom from his princely duties and decorum – and this is certainly intensi-fied by the space in which he resides. Critics and theatregoers over the years may have noticed that Hamlet wants to break free figuratively and from the surrounding autocracy, but they have hardly noticed that he wants literal freedom from this living space: a castle built as a fortress.

Shakespeare even gives us a clue: Claudius orders him to stay – "bend you to remain / Here" (1.2.115–16) – in contrast with allowing Laertes to leave moments earlier. But the figurative imprisonment that Hamlet feels is intensi-fied by the literal confinement of the space. The gates of this vast building are a reminder that Hamlet is also prisoner to his princely birth and the expectations associated with that.

Figure 2.1 Kronborg Castle, 2019 (Islam Issa).

For him, freedom of expression becomes key. So, when he's not in public, he switches his speech to prose rather than decorated verse, proving that decorum and rhetoric are themselves performances: "Now I am alone. / O, what a rogue and peasant slave am I!" (2.2.481–81). The banquet hall where Hamlet's initial interactions with his mother and uncle should take place is a surprisingly large, rectangular room (the size of a football field) with a lofty ceiling; the setting is ceremoniously decorated. Hamlet is, in his description of the world's pomp, also prisoner to the material world. It is no surprise, then, that he ends up finding his freedom of expression through artistic freedom, through theatre. First, when he acts that he is mad (which allows him to disregard etiquettes), and second, when he directs actors for the mousetrap play (which not only allows him to express himself artistically, but also to mix with commoners).

In fact, the result explains why Hamlet is emphatically memorable. He mirrors us, not only in our own forms of daily acting. We have our own differing daily personae when we are at work compared to home. Our interactions on social media, for instance, can bring about another persona in how we articulate ourselves, or what we choose to post (or not), and which photograph we decide to filter and share. On top of that, or perhaps part of that, we are prisoners of society's expectations of who we are and how we should behave: prisoners of certain economic models and of consumerism, expected to fit into a working system and routine, amass debts, dwell in insular nuclear families, and keep up with the latest trends and technologies. Maybe we, too, need to find our own releases.

As is well-known, Hamlet's hesitance to act has been read in several ways. From the indecisive but thus unambivalent hero (serving as a comment on our relationships and problems with authority), to the moral contemplator (serving as a Romantic archetype, especially for conscientious objectors and political quietists), to the psychologically complex, oedipal character championed by Sigmund Freud and his biographer Ernest Jones.

Though psychoanalytic character readings have developed weight, their danger, in the salient words of the Harvard psychiatrist Bennett Simon, is that they place the "moral onus ... on the individual character, and not on the world of other actors and agents who surround him or her".[3] The Shakespearean play is a complex being and much as new criticism moved the debate beyond character analysis, appreciating Hamlet's trauma can help to tie the loose ends that link this fictional character to the undeniable processes and influences of the play's composition and reception. This way, Hamlet can be read less insularly: as a character within an intricate world of plot and setting, and as one who rings true to so much outside the world of the play. This is fitting given that Shakespeare not only peppered *Hamlet* with metatheatrical moments but put metatheatre at the centre of the play. The mousetrap scene is not only about a play within the play, but about an actor playing Hamlet who is simultaneously acting that he is mad, acting like a prince, and acting like a commoner, while actors are playing players and audience members are playing their own personal roles. In addition to the metatheatre, we must also face the fact that the cultural influence of the play, or the *work*, is arguably more weighty than the *text* itself. Hamlet's trauma links him to our present world. After all, trauma and literature are so often connected – so much of what we read has been stimulated by traumatic events: in the last century alone, these include writing about war, and responses to such oppressions as gender politics, racial inequality, colonisation, and the Holocaust. The link with trauma is a factor that makes these works significant and striking. And the literature of terrorism can fall into this category of trauma-linked writing. In Hamlet's case, it confirms his relevance to our societies today, ones that are undoubtedly affected in one way or another by terrorism.[4]

Simon lists some of the key effects of trauma, all of which match Hamlet's state of mind and actions. These include "difficulty in deciding whether what is going on is real" and "interpretation of events becom[ing] constricted or chaotic or both". Hamlet has difficulty understanding whether the Ghost is real or imagined, whether to believe or disregard what he hears, and eventually, whether he himself is mad or not. The result is something trauma patients feel regularly:

> The self and the world become loathesome, and a profound
> mistrust of the future sets in. In the effort to master
> a trauma, the quest for revenge and a scapegoat are
> commonly seen behaviors.[5]

Again, this couldn't be more true of Hamlet, whose mistrust expands to encompass his love object, Ophelia, and again, his own sense of self. He does not revel in enacting revenge as much as he does in searching for it.

We might do well to remember how Horatio warns, from the very start, that Hamlet "waxes desperate with imagination" (1.4.69), though it's unclear whether this is solely a result of grievance or a more permanent trait. There is little doubt that the events leading up to the first scene of the play – his father's death and his mother's remarriage – might well be traumatic for Hamlet. Perhaps it is the first scene – his father's return as the Ghost – that could result in trauma. Or at the very least, the fourth scene, when he sees the Ghost himself and is told that Claudius is the murderer. At whichever stage the trauma occurs, Hamlet may be suffering from post-traumatic stress disorder (PTSD) for at least most of the play. This is accentuated by the fact that he keeps the Ghost story hidden (making his friends swear not to disclose the event) and, furthermore, that he cannot express his seemingly truer, soliloquised feelings in the public world of the play. Giving the example of a child abuse episode, Simon sums up the severity of this fact for Hamlet neatly: "As trauma theory teaches us, the secrecy and extreme difficulty of telling what has gone on are no less damaging than is the actual deed".[6]

Hamlet is essentially censored, though this may also be self-censorship on his part as he chooses not to vocalise all of his thoughts: "I must hold my tongue" (1.2.159). For the audience, remember, events begin in *medias res*. Hamlet has most likely communicated his sorrow directly beforehand; Claudius tells him not "to persever / In obstinate condolement" (1.1.92–93). But he has decided to stop expressing it. This may be, initially, because of the pressure to act in a princely manner, or because Gertrude and Claudius are losing their patience with his grief. Later, because his real thoughts are not in line with the antic disposition, and because being open could compromise his plans for revenge. But when he ceases to vocalise his thoughts to the other characters, Hamlet also ceases to vocalise his trauma. His unexpressed ideas and unaddressed trauma morph into perspectives about the outside world and at different stages of the play end up manifesting themselves as rage and eventually violence.

This is vital to our understanding not only of the traumatised Hamlet, but also of Hamlet as someone who, as discussed, feels that his freedom of expression is compromised. Like many terrorists, his trauma is coupled with attempts to find a way of expressing himself beyond the societal constraints that stop him from doing so – in large part because his thoughts could upset the system.

In fact, the final scene proves that Hamlet is entirely concerned with the fact that he cannot tell his side of the story.[7] As Peter C. Herman puts it, terrorism is "unspeakable" since terrorists wish to outdo themselves and because we "lack the terms to comprehend" the devastation.[8] Hamlet appears to know that he has committed a terroristic act but this makes him uneasy: he wants his actions to be speakable. Perhaps Hamlet's soliloquies overshadow his final speeches. Many people are able to recall the last utterances of Julius Caesar,

Richard III, Romeo, and Juliet, but despite the character's cultural weight, would struggle to recollect any of Hamlet's (and we shall return to the importance of the final Act towards the end of this chapter). Claudius is killed, Hamlet is wounded and taking his last breaths – now, he abhors the traumatised silence he could not overcome during his last days and his most dominant lexical group is concerned almost obsessively with expression:

> I am dead, Horatio. – Wretched queen, adieu! –
> You that look pale and tremble at this chance,
> That are but *mutes* or audience to this act,
> Had I but time – as this fell sergeant, death,
> Is strict in his arrest – O, I could *tell* you. –
> But let it be. – Horatio, I am dead:
> Thou liv'st: *report* me and my causes right
> To the unsatisfied.
>
> (5.2.279–86; emphasis mine).

Hamlet wants Horatio to live in order to tell the story. Hamlet uses similar language to the Ghost's "If thou didst ever thy dear father love" (1.5.27) to, likewise, keep himself alive through expression:

> If thou didst ever hold me in thy heart,
> Absent thee from felicity awhile,
> And in this harsh world draw thy breath in pain,
> To *tell* my story.
>
> (5.2.294–97; emphasis mine).

In his own death, Hamlet knows that silence will ensue, but even so, he wants to express himself to Fortinbras, the next king:

O, I die, Horatio:
The potent poison quite o'er-crows my spirit.
I cannot live to hear the news from England,
But I do prophesy th'election lights
On Fortinbras: he has my dying *voice*,
So *tell* him, with the occurrents more and less
Which have solicited. The rest is *silence*.

      (5.2.301–07; emphases mine)

It is actually ironic that the common perception of Hamlet is that he talks a lot. Artist Mya Gosling's entertaining three-panel caricatures of Shakespeare's plays offer a case in point: the first panel, "Ghost of Hamlet's father tells Hamlet to revenge him", the second, "Hamlet talks a lot about revenging his father", the third, "Hamlet revenges his father". The middle panel confirms the irony. The soliloquies, of course, were in solitude; the audience happens to be there. The *mise-en-scène* movie versions demonstrate this aptly through voice-over, suggesting internal monologue. Laurence Olivier (1948), Grigori Kozintsev (1964), and Michael Almereyda (2000) all incorporate voice-over for the soliloquies. In Olivier, some parts are uttered aloud and some only in Hamlet's mind, while in Kozintsev's Russian film, all of the soliloquies are through voice-over and Hamlet is not always alone during them, emphasising that though he upholds a public profile, his thoughts are private. Such a reading is evident in the text itself, too. When Hamlet complains about his mother's marriage, though the soliloquy is emphatic, he ends it with confirmation that these will remain his private, not public thoughts: "But break my heart, for I must hold my tongue" (1.2.159).

Hamlet might be the Shakespearean character with the most lines in a single play, but he does not talk too much: he

Freedom and principled violence

does not talk enough. Hamlet's seven soliloquies – his truer thoughts (and I say truer, not true, since some follow his antic disposition which he may or may not be internalising) – form no more than 14 percent of the character's lines. In the remaining 1,354 lines, how true is he being to himself? Not very: he tries to fit different persona (whether prince or commoner), actively suppresses his thoughts around others, and feigns madness.

That being said, the soliloquies indicate a mind that cannot stay still: a common root of anxiety. Some of the basic teachings of mindfulness involve training the mind to stay quiet, with some meditation techniques not even permitting meditation until the mind has been trained to stopped thinking, usually by observing one's breath. For the spiritual teacher Eckhart Tolle, author of *The Power of Now*, identifying with one's mind and having a noisy mind are main obstacles to inner peace. Hamlet's internality is evidence of a noisy mind and the longer his trauma goes unaddressed, the longer it engrains itself in him, and the more likely it is to manifest itself problematically. Hamlet's final speeches are also a reminder of his isolation both in life and death. Admitting that he could not express himself during life, Hamlet tries to use death as a means to expression. Though he realises that inevitably "the rest is silence", his last moments indicate a desire to achieve significance through death. This notion alone, in fact, shares a clear similarity with suicide bombers. It also appears to make a case for the utilisation of talk therapy as a tool for countering radicalisation (something the Malaysian government is attempting presently).

In *Much Ado About Nothing*, Don John hardly says anything. He even admits this in his first utterance, when challenged about his loyalty: "I am not of many words, but I thank you" (1.1.105). Unlike Iago's "I am not what I am", Don John is a straight-talking character: "I cannot hide what I am", he says, "I am a plain-dealing villain" (1.3.8–9, 21). He accepts that his illegitimate status cannot be changed but refuses to contemplate either the rationale or end goal of his villainy – or whether he really must be a villain at all. In the world of this comedy, the characters who win out are the ones who speak, who dupe one another and engage in wordplay. In a way, Don John is the least deceiving character in the play. He might be a villain, but he's a rather passive one.

In *Othello*, Iago's pretext for villainy is admittedly loose and far from objective, yet he uses his own imagination and makes a swift decision about the action he will take:

> I know not if't be true,
> But I, for mere suspicion in that kind,
> Will do as if for surety.
>
> (1.3.377–79)

Iago has already decided on his villainy and the second soliloquy is no more than a make-believe contemplation about a decision he has already made, as confirmed by what I read as a whispering aside (and in the printed text of the First Folio, these dashes are actually parentheses):

> The Moor – howbeit that I endure him not –
> Is of a constant, loving, noble nature,
> And I dare think he'll prove to Desdemona
> A most dear husband.
>
> (2.1.272–75)

The motives for Iago's malevolence, including the possibility of Othello cuckolding him, are frankly unconvincing.

Perhaps surprisingly, the closest character to Iago may be Leontes, from *The Winter's Tale*. Leontes has to engage his imagination throughout in order to act in the way that he does. Rather than rational thinking, Leontes creates an obsessive world inside his mind where wife Hermione and best friend Polixenes (the king of Bohemia) are having an affair. As a result, he tries to poison his closest friend (simultaneously an act of regicide), imprisons his wife, casts away his infant daughter, and kills his son through grief.

Also similar to Iago, Richard uses his distress with physical appearance to justify his actions in the very opening scene of *Richard III*. The famous declaration, "I am determined to prove a villain", must be read as two lines since he qualifies it paratactically with: "And hate the idle pleasures of these days". For Richard, love is out because he cannot dance, dogs bark as he passes by, everyone else is pairing off merrily, laughing and joking, while he is limping and grumbling in boredom. Some sympathy is due, but it is hardly convincing rationale to become a child-killing mass murderer. Granted, in these soliloquies, Richard speaks to and for himself, and as Freud realised, for us too: the character opens up about a personal issue related to relationships and self-confidence that some of us may identify with. In a way, he is an ugly version of us. But like Don John, Iago, and Leontes, Richard is still not quite the contemplative, rational actor that Hamlet is.

Hamlet is Shakespeare's greatest play because it asks so many questions. It even begins with one: "Who's there?" (1.1.1). Hamlet is Shakespeare's greatest *character* because he asks so many questions. His interrogation of the human condition makes him the ultimate protagonist. He has an ability to bring the biggest questions to life suddenly: "What a piece of work is a man!" (2.2.284). He knows the power of the mind and its constructions, since "there is nothing either good or bad but thinking makes it so" (2.2.244–45). He knows that what we project might not be who we really are, since "one may smile and smile and be a villain" (1.5.114). He knows that we might shift and change in order to reach what we desire: "I must be cruel, only to be kind" (3.4.176).

Hamlet's insights are in specific contrast to the clichéd and rather unrealistic advice that the king's counsellor, Polonius, gives to his son Laertes: "to thine own self be true" and in turn, "Thou canst not then be false to any man" (1.3.81, 83). What would being true to oneself entail for Hamlet? Acting in a more princely manner, as his mother and uncle suggest, and ignoring perceived injustice? Or would it more simply mean attacking his uncle to avenge his father at the very first opportunity? Even if we interpret Polonius' advice more realistically, it becomes a distressing call for lack of ambition and contemplation, to play the role we've been assigned by society – rather unhelpful for second-class citizens, or in Hamlet's case, someone who is feeling confined, oppressed, and anxious.

From the very start, Hamlet's trusted friend Horatio only "in part" believes the Ghost story: "So have I heard and do in part believe it". In part. We can read the play and particularly Hamlet's thoughts in that light, as demonstrators of an in part reality and mentality:

> What piece of work is a man! How noble in reason, how infinite in faculty, in form and moving how express and admirable, in action how like an angel, in apprehension how

like a god! The beauty of the world, the paragon of animals
– and yet, to me, what is this quintessence of dust?

(2.2.264–67)

Hamlet is noting that humans are in part human. We are also in part god-like: we know hidden truths, we attempt to sway destiny. We're also angel-like and the finest of animals. But, and it's a big but, we will all ultimately turn to dust. The same ending as that skull Hamlet holds, of Yorick, the humble clown. Not just us, though: noble people like Julius Caesar and Alexander the Great, too: "Alexander died, Alexander was buried, Alexander returneth into dust … Imperious Caesar, dead and turned to clay" (5.1.158–59, 161). There's some truth to this: Hamlet's is a message of humility and realism.

Why does all of this matter? Simply, Hamlet ignites questions of what it means to be a human. It is most normal to be in part something and in part something else. Hamlet confirms that the complete human is multidimensional, that identity is multifarious. This struggle extends to his process of decision-making.

When the society around him refuses to take note of his complexity, Hamlet requires a release. He attempts to find this in the form of acting: he directs a play and puts on, it seems, different personae (prince, commoner, avenger, madman). This artistic link may be an added reason for his procrastination, since he attempts to perfect an apt outward image, not only of himself as avenger, but of the very act of revenge. Ruth Nevo calls the moment Hamlet decides against killing Claudius in the chapel the "taint of a fatal aestheticism".[9] But Hamlet also realises the frailty of the art of acting, describing the world, and indeed the Globe Theatre (with its golden ceiling) under which the actor playing him stands, as nothing but smoky air – unpleasant and even deadly:

> this goodly frame, the earth, seems to me a sterile
> promontory, this most excellent canopy, the air, look you,
> this brave o'erhanging firmament, this majestical roof
> fretted with golden fire, why, it appears no other thing to me
> than a foul and pestilent congregation of vapours.
>
> (2.2.280–84)

Does Hamlet become a more authentic version of himself through acting? Hamlet claims that "I essentially am not in madness, / But mad in craft" (3.4.185–86) and it is near impossible to answer the long-standing question of whether he ends up being consumed by his initially feigned antic disposition.[10] We can wonder, though, whether his acting activities, including the antic disposition, add or reduce the congruency of his self-concept. Today, the arts, including theatre, are used for therapy since they can help increase congruence. In other words, does acting make Hamlet's perception of self come into line with his actual feelings, experiences, and actions?

Undoubtedly, Hamlet's overthinking can be interpreted as problematic. Famously, T. S. Eliot declared that the problem with Hamlet is the character's lack of "objective correlative", defined as "a set of objects, a situation, a chain of events which shall be the formula of that *particular* emotion". Eliot adds that "Hamlet (the man) is dominated by an emotion which is inexpressible, because it is in *excess* of the facts as they appear".[11] Eliot's critique identifies, of course, how Hamlet's grief is complicated. But rereading Hamlet in light of terroristic mentality offers an immediate form of explanation. Terrorists can be lone actors: Hamlet does not require other characters to justify his emotions. And terrorists do not need the objects, situations, and events to justify their emotions to anyone; only to themselves. In that way, their mindsets can become quite easily in excess of the facts since these are combined with a highly personal contemplation (often post-traumatic) that is cemented by perceived ideological discovery and a yearning for symbolism.

Nonetheless, Hamlet's contemplation is understandable. As critic Jonathan Bate points out, everyone in the play speaks in doubles: "the sensible and true avouch of mine own eyes", "the gross and scope of my opinion", "the grace and blush of modesty", and so on. Stage props are also doubles: a pair of rapiers, two skulls. Entrances repeat themselves, like the Ghost appearing twice or Ophelia having two madness scenes. In fact, the plot itself: Hamlet, the son, gets vengeance for his dad's death by killing Polonius, another dad (to Laertes). Hamlet notices this: "by the image of my cause I see / The portraiture of his" (5.2.82–83). In fact, Hamlet realises that the killing of his own dad also looks very similar to the anticipated killing of his uncle: to avenge his father, Hamlet must reenact the initial atrocity of murdering the king and murdering his mother's husband.[12] By appreciating these doubles, we can see how these paradoxes understandably puzzle Hamlet's will and confuse him. It is only right that he spends so long pondering whether to take out Claudius, who is all of uncle, step-dad, and king – especially after being instructed by a Ghost during a post-traumatic period and episode. If you've ever rushed Hamlet to just decide already, you obviously haven't put yourself in his position.

It is no secret that when Hamlet first glimpses his father's Ghost, he wonders, commendably, whether to believe it or not, using a series of paradoxes:

> Angels and ministers of grace defend us!
> Be thou a spirit of health or goblin damned,
> Bring with thee airs from heaven or blasts from hell,
> Be thy intents wicked or charitable,
> Thou com'st in such a questionable shape
>
> (1.4.20–24)

Classical avengers would simply seek revenge immediately, but Hamlet is more complex. He wonders, in fact, whether the initial atrocity ever really occurred, fearing that the story may be a trap from the devil. The mousetrap play he puts on plunges him into yet more confusion. And once he does convince himself to avenge, he is confronted by the second phase, to construct himself as an avenger. But he's more like one of us would probably be: attempting to delay the deed for as long as possible. He won't kill his mother in one scene – "O heart, lose not thy nature; … I will speak daggers to her, but use none" (3.3.336, 339) – and in the next, stands over the helpless king, sword in hand, only to hesitate.

The contemplative hesitance and the attempt to rationalise any decisive action make it even more important to consider the question: what is it that makes Hamlet finally switch?

INSPIRED BY IDEOLOGY. CONCERNED WITH SYMBOLISM. ULTIMATELY VIOLENT.

After encountering the Ghost, Hamlet is indecisive about the next step, saying he "*May* sweep to … revenge" (1.5.35;

emphasis mine). But when the Ghost departs with a command of "Hamlet: remember me" (1.5.96), the prince hyperbolically vows to forget everything he knows so that he may do so:

> Remember thee?
> Ay, thou poor ghost, while memory holds a seat
> In this distracted globe. Remember thee?
> Yea, from the table of my memory
> I'll wipe away all trivial fond records,
> All saws of books, all forms, all pressures past
> That youth and observation copied there;
> And thy commandment all alone shall live
> Within the book and volume of my brain,
> Unmixed with baser matter: yes, yes, by heaven!
>
> (1.5.100–09)

Hamlet does not actually set out to take revenge. As he repeats adamantly, Hamlet will remember (or remember to remember) his father, but there is no real promise of revenge at this stage, at least not believably. As John Kerrigan explains, unlike the usual protagonists of revenge tragedy, Hamlet is not as adamant about vengeance as he is about remembrance – to the extent that the latter stifles the former.[13] First, this emphasis in Hamlet's immediate reaction paves the way for the ensuing contemplations about whether to take revenge. Second, it renders his eventual decision to actually take (violent) action in need of some explanation.[14]

Ideology is not only about social or political stances and pejoratives. As leading theorist of ideology Michael Freeden explains, it can also link to the system of frameworks and ideas that people use "in perceiving, comprehending and evaluating" their "realities in general". Ideology can be formed by adding "value-laden meanings into conceptualizations of the social world which are inevitably indeterminate, and is consequently a means of constructing rather than reflecting that world".[15]

Hamlet becomes fuelled by an ideological drive that causes the switch. It is triggered by memory. In order to take action, Hamlet must stop remembering. Should the "remember thee" duo be interpreted as a question or an exclamation? It is in the First Folio (1623) that those familiar question marks make an appearance. The first full version of the play, its Second Quarto (1604), only shows commas after "remember thee".[16] If Hamlet's expression is a question, it signals rhetorically the difficulty of forgetting, which will enable him to remember the Ghost's instruction. If it is not categorically a question, it signals a vow to forget, again enabling him to remember the instruction. But as Rhodri Lewis notes, trying to forget "might be hastened by illness, drugs, the passage of time, or a newly consuming passion, but it cannot be induced by an act of will". But to reach "the mnemonic oblivion that Hamlet describes, there would in reality be only one option open to him: taking his own life".[17] Indeed, trying to forget can lead to suicide. Hamlet tries to remember so stays alive, but the more he realises that to do so he can and must forget, the more he wills to risk his own life. The Ghost is not the one keeping Hamlet alive by giving him the purpose of remembering. Instead, Hamlet is led to a place where he forgets, which essentially serves as an ideological justification to become a killer who is prepared to die.

Incidentally, that Hamlet holds a skull while contemplating death is itself confirmation of his concern with symbolism. This concern is a result of the first scenes of the play, in which Hamlet is not given the platform to remember his father. The suppression confirms to him that remembering in private is not going to be enough. Contrary to the view popularised by Stephen Greenblatt, mourning is not the central issue or motivation and neither is the ability to come to terms with one's own quiet death.[18] Without a public, likely symbolic act, how effective can remembrance be? The most symbolic thing Hamlet does is to kill and be killed. G. Wilson Knight has argued that Hamlet's confusion about the nature and significance of life, as well as his creative confinement, means that "[n]o act but suicide is rational". For Hamlet, then, some sort of suicide appears to be inevitable. However, he then receives a lifeline in "the command of a great act—revenge".[19] This enables him to place suicide and revenge hand in hand so that revenge becomes all the more symbolic through his own death.

The Ghost tells Hamlet to take revenge but says his farewell before asking to be remembered: "Adieu, adieu, Hamlet: remember me" (1.5.96). Remembrance is almost an afterthought. In Hamlet's immediate comprehension and evaluation of the encounter, the practical and determinate demand of revenge is outweighed by the more indeterminate idea of remembrance. It is Hamlet who tries to turn the Ghost's final utterance into something meaningful and determinate that he will achieve through forgetting. By responding in this way, Hamlet begins to build his own systemic framework – forget, remember, avenge. In turn, he *constructs* rather than *reflects* a world that is based on this encounter. Without realising, Hamlet's own reality is now driven by ideology.

The theme of memory has a significant presence in Renaissance literature and *Hamlet* is a prime instance.[20] But for Hamlet specifically, forgetting and remembering are the driving forces of his *ideological* formation. Contemplation coupled with ideology is what differentiates Hamlet from other heroes of the stage like Thomas Kyd's Hieronimo. The introductory chapter to this book noted the importance of Bin Laden's memory to the formation and articulation of his views, as well as the influence that the conception of and desire for a nostalgic past has on alt-right and religiously fanatic terrorists. It is true that *Hamlet* is about the past – and this is something which matches aspects of its protagonist's thinking with the terrorist mindset.

As Emma Smith notes in her convincing reading of *Hamlet*, the play's "religious historiography" possesses a clear "nostalgic pull". It shows "theatrical" nostalgia by objecting to boy actors and reminiscing about Kyd's *Spanish Tragedy* and the Tudor interludes: "like the time of old Hamlet, of Yorick, or Priam, of Hieronimo, things, the play says, were better in the past".[21] Even Hamlet's name, the same as his father's, "pulls him backwards into previous plays and previous generations". The Ghost therefore serves to symbolise "the past: familial, political, cultural and temporal", while the fact that Hamlet's father has died prior to events on the stage creates a past that is already "unreachable, a place beyond the compass of the play".[22]

Not only are memory and nostalgia important to terrorists, but their mindset is also concerned with retaliation and response – to a divergent ideology, an alleged injustice, or a specific event. Rather than advance their own causes practically, they might be satisfied merely stifling those of the enemy. In most cases, then, terrorists are attempting to undo rather than to do. Smith summarises this neatly in relation to Hamlet: that his actions cause more "negation" than "progress".[23] What is more, terrorists tend to have role models from the past, most often deceased, and in trying to get revenge for those who have died before them, they become attached to those who have passed on. Again, Smith's summary that Hamlet's "primary attachments are to the dead not the living" hits the nail on the head.[24] Hamlet's concern with the past and its dislocation, then, identifies him with a key facet of terrorist mentality. This is further intensified through his own ideological formation as well as an emphasis on religion. Read in context, Hamlet's "looking backward not forward is related to religion" since Hamlet represents the anxieties of the Reformation as "a Protestant son haunted by the ghost of a Catholic father".[25] This can be extended to the juncture in which he is operating: one in which social and moral changes are taking place that he is struggling to navigate and that require him to hold onto the old way of doing things.[26]

How does the fact that memory is at the core of the play change Hamlet's actions? Should we see his flip into violence and death coming? Even in our own lives, the transition from thinking to acting cuts across a fine line. In the context of a play, this is the transition from words to action, not least from soliloquy to action (in Hamlet's case, it's a devastating transition since action leads to fatality). Perhaps all one needs to actually carry out a thought is a moment of self-realisation – or self-delusion. In other words, I propose that the act of remembering is not a hint towards counter-vengeance. Remembering is in fact the first step towards vengeance. It's why terrorists are inundated with images and reminders of the atrocities apparently committed against their people over history. That is why the Ghost emphasises memory – and it works.

Hamlet ends up trying to see his past through his own death. In this way, he becomes akin to the terrorists who film their death messages. They use their anticipation of the future moment to define their actions and to retrospectively rewrite their history. They respond to their past through death.

One might even argue that *Hamlet* is as much about the future as the past. After all, Hamlet spends much of the play pondering what he will do and what the consequences of any action will be. His overriding concern with the afterlife – which stops him from killing Claudius – shows how a perception of the future dictates his actions. That moment has been open to numerous interpretations and seemed tactful to me until I visited the chapel on the Kronborg Castle grounds. As I heard the heavy door shutting behind me and my footsteps echoing ominously, my immediate thought was that Claudius would be sitting at that altar trying to repent. That is Hamlet's clearest opportunity to kill Claudius, but by choosing not to commit the deed while the king is in prayer, Hamlet proves that he doesn't just want revenge, he wants Claudius to be damned, forever. Hamlet, here, is at his most vengeful. Samuel Johnson realised this two and a half centuries before me: "This speech, in which Hamlet, represented as a virtuous character, is not content with taking blood for blood, but contrives damnation for the man that he would punish, is too horrible to be read or to be uttered".[27]

Hamlet's concern with the future is telling. He aspires to create a utopian world and bases his decisions on hypotheses about the afterlife. So often, terrorists talk about the future. This involves the utopian world they aspire to create. It also involves the afterlife, a concept which gives extra incentive to their actions: both the bliss they believe they will be rewarded with and the wrath that their enemies will face. Emphasis on the afterlife is most often through a religious lens.

When Hamlet describes the setting and life situation as "a prison", a phrase that only appears in the Folio version, it is the first step towards signalling his own death. Roman and Christian writings have long been concerned with martyrdom and more generally present death as freedom. Seneca the Younger and Boethius, for instance, refer to death as *liberum* and *libera*; the latter specifies that it is from the *terreno carcere* or "earthly prison". Similarly, in *A Dialogue of Comfort against Tribulation*, Thomas More (who, in the twentieth century, would become canonised as a Catholic martyr) writes of escaping earthly "imprisonment" to heavenly "lybertie".[28]

Belief in an afterlife can be a positive influence for some people. But it can also be important in a terrorist's narrative of self-justification. Indeed, afterlife is also a key facet in the concept of martyrdom, which over history has been important to most major faith groups, particularly the Abrahamic faiths and Sikhism. But to suffer or die for a devoted cause is often coupled with the promise of a fitting and idyllic reward for the sacrifice.

Richard Wilson has argued that Shakespeare's own biographical context in which his Catholic friends and family were being persecuted proves that his works, by being "resistant to [the] resistance" of fervent Catholics, "made a drama out of his refusal of a terror" and more specifically made his works "critiques of martyrdom".[29] Later in this book, we will consider the role of Shakespeare's own context, particularly in relation to the plots against Queen Elizabeth and the Gunpowder Plot of 1605, both of which had direct links to his home county of Warwickshire. A biographical historicisation of *Hamlet* is certainly useful, though whether it is as clear-cut as Wilson and before him Richard Simpson make out remains open to debate. Nonetheless, it usefully points towards the way in which Hamlet is not an idealised hero: he is an example of just one possible ideology, one possible reaction, method, and course of action. Despite Hamlet's best efforts, what he ends up opting for is hard to justify and at best only rudimentarily successful. Perhaps we feel otherwise because the final word is reserved for Hamlet's friend Horatio: the only person with whom Hamlet has shared his newfound ideology and who is convinced that Hamlet is going to heaven: "Goodnight, sweet prince, / And flights of angels sing thee to thy rest!" (5.2.308–09).

Indeed, Hamlet justifies his violent switch using religion. Think of that famous image of Hamlet carrying the skull in the very last Act. In addition to perhaps having yet more time, off stage, to contemplate during his travels, Hamlet now approaches death differently. His presence in the graveyard is a moment in which he sees and touches physical manifestations of death and becomes a trigger for his eventual actions. It might appear that Hamlet kills Claudius in a rash moment despite spending the play contemplating death. But that rashness is the result of an ideological development and a far from rash choice to be rash. He has already killed Polonius in the spur of the moment in his mother's chamber. In the graveyard, Hamlet cements the idea that life and death are actually out of his control. This sets his mindset into the exact mode he had required all along: in trusting fate, he becomes desensitised to the idea of killing so that when the opportunity arises shortly later, he is able to act in the moment, separating himself and his action in order to act submissively and out of the parameters of his normal hesitant or moral character. To reach this state, he develops a new spiritual mode. He uses faith and God to justify a divinely inspired rashness:

> Rashly –
> And praise be rashness for it – let us know
> Our indiscretion sometime serves us well,
> When our deep plots do pall, and that should teach us
> There's a divinity that shapes our ends,
> Rough-hew them how we will–
>
> (5.2.6–11)

Taking matters spontaneously into one's own hands is part of God's plan and in turn becomes a justifiable mode of action. In an outstanding piece of literary criticism, Fernie has shown how the significance of Hamlet's "last act" is too often overlooked. Fernie goes as far as summarising that "the thing that actually converts Hamlet to violence is something like a religious epiphany", adding:

> When Hamlet starts talking about God and metaphysics he starts praising rashness, and he starts seeing action flowing through him – and he sees himself as an agent of God in the final act when he becomes a murderous avenger.[30]

By committing to God, Hamlet is able to "combine the violence of a specific commitment with the assurance of doing right".[31] The clarity of his belief at this stage informs a newfound willingness "not to be" (and can be curiously juxtaposed with Caesar's and Mandela's assured acceptance of mortality). The commitment and clarity allow Hamlet to reframe and redefine his potential death, which he had rejected in the form of suicide, as martyrdom. Moreover, his endorsement of a divine rashness gives him the ability to act violently without contemplating the wider consequences. Like so many terrorists, his single action will end up creating a pileup of bodies at the scene.

Describing Claudius' letter to Horatio, Hamlet notes he is under threat: they see "such bugs and goblins in my life" (5.2.23). To Claudius, Hamlet is a terrorist or terror suspect. And despite Hamlet's own contemplations suggesting a more principled violence, he remains on the terrorist wanted list. Essentially, the letter notes the terror that will exist should Hamlet live. Here, Shakespeare enables us to foresee the eventual bloodbath.

EPILOGUE: THE PARADOX OF FREEDOM

Even Shakespearean characters we do not associate immediately with terror might be more terroristic than we think. Recognition of Hamlet's potentially terroristic traits might not be new, but such a viewpoint has not been dominant in general critical reception or popular consciousness.

Hamlet's strife might be instigated by the Ghost's appearance, but it had already begun in his longing for freedom. Remember, "nobody wakes up or is born a terrorist; it's a long term process, it's gradual".[32] By turning this strife into extreme action, he presents more clearly the paradox of freedom. Fernie puts it neatly when he defines freedom as "the virtue that entails at least the possibility of evil".[33] In theory, whatever freedoms we claim, we should also grant. But over history, societies and individuals – including terrorist organisations and indeed governments – have been prepared to limit the freedoms of others for the sake of their own freedoms. Note the criminologist Awan's statement that "the common theme for" terrorists is "that they are seeking that principle of freedom at all costs".[34] Hamlet notices the paradoxes associated with his actions: "by the image of my cause I see / The portraiture of his" (5.2.82–83). When it comes to tolerance and freedom of speech, the predicament is particularly tricky: should free speech extend to those who wish to incite hatred or to eliminate these principles?

The moral implications are vast but manifest themselves in real historical moments. Philosopher Erich Fromm, a German Jew who fled the Nazis, categorised freedom as either "from" something or "to" something. To have "freedom from", he argued, is not in itself a sufficient or gratifying experience, unless it is coupled with a "freedom to". As a result, many people end up coupling "freedom from" with one of three characteristics: authoritarianism, destructiveness, or conformity.[35] All three of these link to terrorist mentality. When a terrorist seeks "freedom from" but does not understand the responsibilities associated with "freedom to", they may become an authoritarian figure (like Hitler or Bin Laden), a destructive figure (like Nazi guards or a suicide bomber) or a conformist (like cooperative or complicit citizens who rationalised Nazi actions, or an al-Qaeda member). And Hamlet – who cannot find the "freedom to" express himself, grieve, travel, and enact justice – falls into these traps the moment he seeks his own freedom at the expense of others. He begins to make authoritarian decisions, to be destructive, and indeed to conform to the expectations of a revenge hero. The death of others becomes more tolerable and justified as a means towards achieving his own freedom, which can itself be through his own death.

To terrorists, such acceptance of violence might appear principled. But violence is violence. We might differentiate terror from other types of violence by what comes before it: the contexts, rationales, and symbolisms. These are most often externally dictated: by the leaders, media, and the operating narratives. As a result, the perpetrators can tend to be the instruments not the agents, matching Johnson's famous rebuke that "Hamlet is, through the whole play, rather an instrument than an agent".[36]

We might still choose to sign on to the perception of a moral, sensitive, withholding Hamlet, and put him – and in turn our own ideals of canonical culture and literature – on the right side of history. But this choice is not without its complications. As well as having terroristic traits, Hamlet's afterlife is also mixed. Whether or not he is an instrument in the play is open to question. That he has been utilised by some extremists as an instrument to justify their actions is a matter of fact.

NOTES

1 Ewan Fernie, *Shakespeare for Freedom: Why the Plays Matter* (Cambridge: Cambridge University Press, 2017), 18.
2 It is worth noting that Viola also uses this phrase while disguised as Cesario in *Twelfth Night* (3.2.122). I am indebted to Ewan Fernie for alerting me to the wider resonance of Iago's phrase. See also Ewan Fernie, *The Demonic: Literature and Experience* (London: Routledge, 2012), 3–9; emphases mine.
3 Bennett Simon, "Hamlet and the Trauma Doctors: An Essay at Interpretation", *American Imago* 58.3 (Fall 2001), 707–22, 708.
4 There have also many readings of Hamlet's mental state; see Nicolas Brémauda, "Hamlet and Madness: A Historical Review", *L'Évolution Psychiatrique* 80.1 (2015), 164–86.
5 Simon, "Hamlet and the Trauma Doctors", 712.
6 Ibid., 716; emphasis mine.
7 Ibid., 718.
8 Herman, *Unspeakable*, 5–6.
9 Ruth Nevo, *Tragic Form in Shakespeare* (Princeton: Princeton University Press, 1972), 162.
10 This has, of course, long been a subject of debate, including such publications as *The Hamlet Controversy. Was Hamlet Mad? Or, The*

Freedom and principled violence

Lucubrations of Messrs. Smith, Brown, Jones, and Robinson (Melbourne: H. T. Dwight, 1867).

11 T. S. Eliot, "Hamlet and His Problems" in The Sacred Wood (London, 1920), 92.

12 Jonathan Bate, "Introduction", in William Shakespeare, Hamlet, ed. Jonathan Bate and Eric Rasmussen (Basingstoke: Macmillan, 2008), 2.

13 John Kerrigan, "Hieronimo, Hamlet and Remembrance", Essays in Criticism 31.2 (1981): 105–26, 113–14, 118–19. On Hamlet's speech, see Garrett Sullivan, Memory and Forgetting in English Renaissance Drama (Cambridge: Cambridge University Press, 2005), 13–15.

14 Rhodri Lewis makes a compelling case that shows how this remembrance is actually "never the force that Hamlet works so hard to make it seem"; see Rhodri Lewis, "Hamlet, Metaphor, and Memory", Studies in Philology 109.5 (2012): 609–41, 635.

15 Michael Freeden, "Ideology", Routledge Encyclopedia of Philosophy (Taylor and Francis, 1998), www.rep.routledge.com/articles/thematic/ideology/v-1 [accessed 1 November 2019].

16 The question marks in the Folio look very clear, though it could also be worth mentioning that some early modern printing complicates this by placing question marks in place of exclamation points.

17 Lewis, "Hamlet, Metaphor, and Memory", 629–30.

18 See Stephen Greenblatt, Hamlet in Purgatory (Princeton: Princeton University Press, 2001).

19 G. Wilson Knight, The Wheel of Fire: Interpretations of Shakespearian Tragedy (London: Methuen, 1986), 19–20.

20 See Hester Lees-Jeffries, Shakespeare and Memory (Oxford: Oxford University Press, 2013); Andrew Hiscock, Reading Memory in Early Modern Literature (Cambridge: Cambridge University Press, 2010). On the political, see Kyle Pivetti, Of Memory and Literary Form: Making the Early Modern English Nation (Lanham: University of Delaware Press, 2015).

21 Emma Smith, "Hamlet", Approaching Shakespeare Podcast, https://podcasts.ox.ac.uk/hamlet (2012); on theatrical memory, see Peter Holland, ed. Shakespeare, Memory and Performance (Cambridge: Cambridge University Press, 2006).

22 Emma Smith, This Is Shakespeare: How to Read the World's Greatest Playwright (London: Pelican, 2020), 165–66.

23 Ibid., 167.

24 Ibid.

25 Smith, "Hamlet"; Smith, *This Is Shakespeare*, 180. On this reading of Hamlet, see Greenblatt, *Hamlet in Purgatory*.

26 See James Shapiro, *A Year in the Life of William Shakespeare* (London: Faber & Faber, 2011), 276–78.

27 Samuel Johnson, ed. *The Plays of William Shakespeare*, vol. 7 (London, 1765), 236.

28 Joshua Scodel, "Finding Freedom in Hamlet", *Modern Language Quarterly* 72.2 (2011): 163–200, 180.

29 Richard Wilson, *Secret Shakespeare: Studies in Theatre, Religion and Resistance* (Manchester: Manchester University Press, 2004), ix, 295, 5.

30 Ewan Fernie, in Islam Issa, "Shakespeare and Terrorism", prod. Sara Jane Hall, BBC Radio 3 (4 November 2018), unpublished recording; see also Ewan Fernie, "The Last Act: Presentism, Spirituality and the Politics of *Hamlet*", in *Spiritual Shakespeares*, ed. Ewan Fernie (New York: Routledge, 2005).

31 Fernie, "The Last Act", 204.

32 Imran Awan, in Islam Issa, "Shakespeare and Terrorism", prod. Sara Jane Hall, BBC Radio 3 (4 November 2018).

33 Fernie, *Shakespeare for Freedom*, 77.

34 Awan, in Issa, "Shakespeare and Terrorism", BBC Radio 3; emphasis mine.

35 Erich Fromm, *Escape from Freedom* (New York: Farrar and Rinehart, 1941).

36 Samuel Johnson, *The Yale Edition of the Works of Samuel Johnson: Johnson on Shakespeare*, vol. 7, ed. A. Sherbo (London: Yale University Press, 1968), 1011.

Performing ideology and power

Three

THE CONDUIT OF AVON

Through today, Shakespeare's hometown of Stratford-upon-Avon celebrates his birthday every April. It may well come as a surprise that in the 1939 celebrations, a swastika flag flew over Stratford-upon-Avon in close proximity to the birthplace of Shakespeare. We will return to the story of Stratford's swastika. The previous chapter read terror within the dramatic world of *Hamlet*. This chapter returns to twentieth-century afterlives and refractions of the political dimensions of this play's terror.

In his travel writing, D. H. Lawrence (1885–1930) admits:

> I had always felt an aversion to Hamlet: a creeping,
> unclean thing he seems ... The character is repulsive
> in its conception, based on self-dislike and a spirit of
> disintegration.[1]

The young writer, travelling in his twenties and having attended a performance of *Hamlet* in Italy, acknowledges the protagonist's potential as an antagonist. It is intriguing that Lawrence, in a similar tone to Bin Laden, dislikes this Shakespearean hero. Despite writing a great deal during his short life (dying at 44), Lawrence had written relatively little

DOI: 10.4324/9780429320088-4

at this stage. As is the case with Bin Laden, this opinion of Shakespeare precedes their fame and careers, so this comment might prefigure some of the arguments Lawrence makes later in his life.

If Hamlet is able to inspire extremist ideology, one might expect this to relate to vengeance and violence. But Lawrence's professed loathing of Hamlet is not related to these. It is because of Hamlet's apathy. Lawrence's dislike of sloth is clear in his essay, "Why I Don't Like Living in London" in which he repeatedly dubs everything in the city "dull": "The strange, the grey and uncanny, almost deathly sense of dullness is overwhelming".[2] Actually, this is an equally strong description of Kronborg Castle! Lawrence's emphasis on Hamlet's indecisive nature, rather than violent action, helps to confirm two things. First, that beyond Hamlet's physical violence, the character can still be a contentious and negative figure. Second, in expressing this opinion, Lawrence is himself utilising Shakespeare and Hamlet as conduits for his own concerns.

On the first of these, apart from physical violence, Hamlet is able to influence a mode of ideological vehemence – something that will become apparent in this chapter. In Lawrence's case, disdain for Hamlet's ideological influence manifests itself in the writer's views of the corruptions associated with religion, modern morality, and popular culture. To Lawrence, Hamlet's personality is in line with a view that living in the modern world has created self-loathing, sexually repressed individuals: a shadow of what they could be. In "Pan in America", Lawrence laments humanity's distance from their essential primal and human urges. Hamlet being "unclean" is not the promiscuous impurity that would have been associated with the term, especially due to the influence of the social purity movement in the late nineteenth and early twentieth centuries. Here, to be unclean is to *deny* one's urges and instincts – whether to confront Claudius or to sleep with Ophelia – and to distance oneself from a pure form of life through the corruption of overthinking and being caught in the "trappings" (1.2.86) of the world. Though Lawrence's writings touch on these issues, much as Bin Laden's recollection of encountering Shakespeare as a youngster is recorded in a journal entry just months before his death worked to solidify his worldview, Lawrence only delineates the ideas encapsulated in his early criticism of Hamlet towards the very end of his life in *Pornography and Obscenity*.

There might be personal reasons for Lawrence's views. His dislike of Hamlet could be a reflection of an ambivalent relationship to his non-conformist upbringing or defensiveness about his mother. Indeed, Lawrence showed knowledge of Oedipal relations and took Freud to task for being too prescriptive. The topic bothered him so much that he wrote a novel about it, *Sons and Lovers*, in which he addresses the relationship between girlfriend and mother, reflecting on his own youthful romance with Jessie Chambers. His relationship with Frieda, a German literary figure who was already married and with whom he eloped to Italy at this time also suggests a decisiveness that is antithetical to Hamlet's. Hamlet's objections to a seemingly unorthodox marriage (Gertrude and Claudius) may also have struck a chord with objections to Lawrence's relationships.

Essentially, Lawrence is doing what others do: using Hamlet as a conduit for his own ideas. Importantly, by objecting to Hamlet's rationality and self-awareness, Lawrence agrees indirectly with the more primal actions of the protagonist: in other words, the rashness of Hamlet that leads to extreme action. And if Lawrence reaches this conclusion about Hamlet, then we shouldn't be surprised that extremists can too.

In 2005, Danish television aired a debate between a far-right politician named Mogens Camre and an imam and academic named Fatih Alev. Known for his opposition to Islamist extremism, Alev believes that there is no conflict between Islamic and Danish values. When Camre made a lurid statement about the Muslim faith having much in common with Nazism and Alev responded, neither would have known how the events to follow were to have national and international significance. The newspaper *Jyllands-Posten* invited illustrators to draw cartoons of Muhammad: twelve agreed and two were particularly offensive.[3] One portrayed a man with a bomb for a turban and the other had him exclaiming that heaven has run out of virgins. Aside from aniconistic traditions that limit pictorial depictions of sentient beings, drawing the holiest figure in Islam (second only to Allah) in an offensive manner was bound to cause upset. US President Bill Clinton was among those who condemned the cartoons and countries including Saudi Arabia recalled their ambassadors from Denmark. Protests around the world were mostly peaceful, though some, like the one in London, were led by extremists. Their banners included "Europe you will pay, Bin Laden is on his way" and more bewildering slogans like "Freedom go to hell" and "Freedom of expression go to hell".[4] Ironically, the extremists here used their own freedoms to protest against freedom, again confirming the freedom paradox at play. A serious boycott of Denmark ensued in the Arab region: it became a social offence to buy a Danish product, most notably Arla's popular Puck cheese (a product with the same name as the mythological fairy of *A Midsummer*

Night's Dream since Arabic renditions of the play retain his original name). The company lost $2 million dollars per day for months, even leading to a full-page advert in a Saudi Arabian newspaper that apologised for the cartoons.[5] In the years that followed, several individuals in Denmark and the US have been charged with terrorism-related offences for plotting to attack the newspaper headquarters or individual cartoonists, one of whom has police protection. French magazine *Charlie Hebdo* was one outlet that chose to republish the *Jyllands-Posten* cartoons. The 2015 al-Qaeda gun attacks on the *Charlie Hebdo* offices and a nearby kosher supermarket were in some ways part of the Danish case's aftermath.

Hamlet crept into this controversy consistently. During their sighting of the Ghost, Marcellus utters to Horatio the now well-known phrase: "Something is rotten in the state of Denmark" (1.4.72). It's probably no surprise that this became a recurring phrase during the cartoon controversy. Newspapers in Muslim-majority countries used it over and over: what could be more rotten than insulting the most esteemed human in the religion? One editorial even named and blamed the likes of Bin Laden for marring the image of Islam and in turn leading to such hostile portrayals. One Iraqi newspaper explained that it is the Danish cartoonists who are "extremists".

In turn, the responses questioned freedom of expression. Most notably, some months after these reactions, the *San Francisco Chronicle* published a piece titled "Something Is Rotten Outside the State of Denmark". It argued that there "is a fundamental misunderstanding among many Muslims about the meaning of free speech in the West" and that "political correctness is another of multiculturalism's destructive offshoots".[6] The responses from the Muslim-majority countries, as well as the politicians and journalists of the US, had apparently proved that freedom of speech was being compromised. The article concluded that while Europe has shown that political correctness should not stand in the way of criticising Islam, the US has been too scared to follow suit. Apparently, the rottenness is not only in the Muslim-majority countries, but actually in the US. Fascinatingly, then, the Shakespearean phrase became redeployed repeatedly as part of a clashing cultural back and forth. Beginning as a phrase from the esteemed Western playwright, it became an explication of discontent with Western treatment of Muslims, before being redeployed by Western responses as an indication of the alleged narrow-mindedness of Muslims and the supposedly "apologetic" reactions that followed.

The term "state" could mean multiple things, from the country and government, to the conditions and mindsets. But looking at the Arabic translation of "rotten", often "muta'afin", could lend itself to literal readings. Two things come to mind. Bodies, like the pile of bodies on the stage at the end. Recent research has tried to define the smell of dead bodies, particularly in cases of terrorism and mass graves; in 2012, United Nations monitors described smelling burnt flesh when they arrived in a Syrian town following a massacre by militia forces.[7] The second relates to trash, where in many places around the world, a lack of organised refuse disposal and collection results in a pungent smell. This could be related to incompetent local governments or to a political issue like in Jordan-controlled East Jerusalem, where residents complain about much poorer refuse infrastructure and collection compared to Israel-controlled West Jerusalem.[8] In fact, the relationship between trash and terror is an odd one: more than half of UK councils use anti-terror surveillance cameras to catch people putting their bins out on the wrong day, and in 2017, councils installed safety options to their garbage trucks to stop the risk of terrorists from using them for attacks.[9] But the question being raised here is rather simple: is something – like corpses or trash – actually rotten in Kronborg? If so, Hamlet's response might be building on this context.[10]

The simple fact is that single, simple phrases from Shakespeare – including but by no means limited to "Something is rotten in the state of Denmark" – can serve as conduits for a range of complex ideas. With rising global interconnectedness and digital media, the intertextualities and allusions have reached a kind of meta status, in which the references are no longer to Shakespeare per se but to an earlier usage of the phrase; in the case of the *San Francisco Chronicle*, referring to the Muslim columnists' responses.

Of course, the most famous literary phrase in the English canon is Hamlet's "To be, or not to be" (3.1.62). So it is no surprise that it has been used by an array of people: from those fighting terror to those who instigate it. Again, the Arab world offers some clear examples. Margaret Litvin has noted how the Arabic language translation requires a pronoun due to its lack of infinitive form. While no translators or actors pick the plural, she adds, the phrase's "life as a political slogan" consistently uses the plural.[11] The immediate impact of this is to make Hamlet's personal dilemma into a collective plight and thus one that can be more readily framed and positioned within ideological narratives.

The Islamic *sahwah* (awakening), described in Chapter 1, invigorated a new religious fervour that swept across the Arab region. While it pushed some to become more conscientious and seek to improve their neighbourhoods and societies, it was also a catalyst for *takfīr* (excommunicating someone as a disbeliever), as well as violence: in Algeria, Egypt (the assassination of President Anwar Sadat), Lebanon (the creation of Hezbollah), Palestine (the creation of Hamas), and even some responses in the Salman Rushdie affair.

Egyptian writer Farag Foda (1946–1992) became recognised as one of the vocal critics of the sahwah's tendencies towards nostalgic and political Islam and its popularisation of the Muslim Brotherhood. Foda's views, which related to Islam and called for a separation between civil and religious society, led to accusations of ignorance, blasphemy, and eventually apostasy from figures of religious authority linked to al-Azhar, the world's foremost Sunni institution. Even in the strictest interpretations of Islamic laws, apostasy requires a trial-like event in which numerous steps must be completed. But after some clerics' views were published in a religious newspaper and picked up by extremists, there was going to be trouble.

In 1988, Foda's book *To Be or Not To Be* (in its plural form, *Nakūn aw lā Nakūn*) was published. The collection of articles begins with an introduction that explains indirectly the relevance of the Shakespeare-inspired title. Like much of his work, Foda's book details his thoughts on the ensuing clashes and potential contradictions between modernity and the miscellanies that the sahwah encouraged some religious leaders to pursue, like aspiration for a religious state or the regulation of dress. Hamlet is clearly applicable: after all, he meddles with a range of junctures and clashes such as the forced primacy of Protestantism at the expense of Catholicism, the shift to renaissance humanism, and most personally for him, the paradox between morality (or chivalry) and heroism – all coupled with a confinement of expression. Foda suggests that his book "reflects the reality of the intellectual battles we are living through" and future generations "might not believe that we wrote it while sinking in accusations of apostasy and surrounded by swords of terrorism and threat". Those who read this in the future will do well to remember, he adds, that "they are indebted to us for this [free] climate. And they will discover as they turn our pages while we are a memory, that we paid the price".[12] In 1992, days after the accusatory newspaper article about him, Foda was shot in a targeted assassination by the terrorist organisation *al-Jamāʿah al-Islāmiyyah* (in English, the Islamic Group). They had branched from the Muslim Brotherhood when the latter's leaders renounced violence in the 1970s and in addition to this killing, carried out two of the worst terrorist attacks on tourists in Egypt's modern history. The attackers didn't read Foda's work – in fact, they were illiterate. The same group had even attacked a Greek tour-bus thinking that the writing was in Hebrew. The point is that Foda's allusion to *Hamlet* indicates the volatility of his own context and not only foreshadows his own death, but turns his view on this important point in Egypt's future into a volatile and binary enquiry: civil versus religious. Nonetheless, resurfaced television footage from the 1990s shows Foda arguing that terrorism in the name of Islam will increase and that young, disenfranchised men will retaliate to economic crises by accepting the lure of a violent so-called "Islamic state". Even Foda's critics – and there are many who still consider him a misinformed secularist – might accept that there is some truth in what he predicted. In fact, one of the five sentenced for Foda's murder was freed in 2012 only to join ISIS before being killed in Syria in 2017.[13]

The 1992 assassination of Foda inspired one of the most important Arabic movies of the modern period: *al-Irhābī*, or *The Terrorist* (1994). Starring the region's biggest star, Adel Imam, it depicts a simple, brainwashed terrorist who, after attempting to assassinate a prominent journalist clearly representing Foda, gets run over by a woman and ends up recovering at her house where he sees beyond his extremist bubble into a regular and loving middle-class, moderate Muslim household. The movie is a tragedy, complete with girl meets boy, a rise and fall, and cathartic denouement. When it was released, police were assigned to cinema theatres in order to manage any potential violence. To some, Imam's critical portrayal of extremism was a criticism of pious religious practices. Rather void of nuance, the characters have clearly false beards, furrowed eyebrows, and the content and style of their speeches is stereotypical. As a result of this movie in particular, Imam received numerous death threats through the 1990s, leading to protection and security cordons for years. When in 2012, the Muslim Brotherhood won the presidential elections in Egypt, a lawyer took Imam to court for insulting Islam, primarily citing this movie as well as another classic, *al-Irhāb wal-Kabāb* (*Terrorism and Kebab*). The play *al-Za'īm* (*The Leader*) was also mentioned; in it, Imam satirised numerous dictators, including Libyan Muammar Gaddafi, who allegedly attempted to assassinate him as a result.[14] The Egyptian court charged Imam with "defaming Islam" and sentenced him to three months in prison and a fine, though he soon launched a successful appeal.[15]

Foda's use of Hamlet's phrase as the title for his book is in line with the most common way it has been used by public figures in the region: as a signal towards a common existential crisis affecting a nation or collective nations. One such example is by the late Palestinian leader Yasser Arafat (1929–2004), even more striking because Palestine's relationship with art, Shakespeare included, is so curious. The risk of turning the political debate into a cultural commodity and thereby neutralising it always looms large. A recent example of this was Banksy's ridiculous Walled Off Hotel offering rooms with West Bank Wall views. Can Palestinian culture (including responses to English literature) be anything but political? Does cementing a political or an apolitical Palestinian identity work or is it, either way, a form of co-option? If a Palestinian created the most abstract, apolitical piece, it is still likely to be read in light of the politics. There, Shakespeare is no different: the strife of Romeo and Juliet, from two feuding families, echoes the common love story of a young man on one side of the wall and a young woman on the other side, or even a forbidden Palestinian-Israeli romance. So when Arafat was asked in a 1983 interview about the chances of Arab unity, his use of *Hamlet* was indicative of the blurred line between the personal and the collective, between the political and the artistic. He answered: "Put simply, the Arab leaders must rise to their historical and national responsibilities. It is a simple question for the Arab nations: to be or not to be".[16] Arafat, who had a distinctive rhetorical style in Arabic, also does something surprisingly rare: he recalls that Hamlet's utterance is actually a *question*. The inclusion of the Shakespearean phrase made his answer simultaneously "simple", as he claimed, and entirely complicated. In a way, it is a valid summary of Arab unity.

The activity of quoting in these contexts increased yet more in the aftermath of 9/11, an incident that posed existential questions and became an immediately disruptive moment that threatened to create further splits (West and East; pre-9/11 and post-9/11). Yusuf al-Qaradawi (1926–) is arguably the most influential Sunni scholar of the late twentieth and early twenty-first centuries. Though barred from entering some European countries, he remains a key global authority. At the time of 9/11, he had an audience in the tens of the millions via Al Jazeera television and has generally denounced extremism. His responses to 9/11, then, were important. As Litvin is first to record, one of his immediate written responses was an article titled "Dialogue between Islam and Christianity", in which he condemns terrorism and calls on Muslims to show their true, peaceful colours:

> I confirm to you that we are in a moment that resembles –
> to some extent – the saying, "To be or not to be". So either
> we do something which has meaning and feasibility that
> contributes to directing events in a sound direction in
> accordance to the spirit of the beliefs with which we are
> affiliated; either this or the page of neglect and oblivion has
> turned on us, maybe forever.[17]

This response to 9/11 is significant in that it confirms the gravity not only of a single event but of the responses to it. The terroristic moment creates a change in our own lives whether we are involved directly or not; it certainly did, for instance, for citizens of the US or for Muslims worldwide. Then, our response to that change further defines the impact of the event itself. One could say that in the play, the assassination of King Hamlet and to an extent the appearance of his Ghost are life-changing events for the characters, not least for Prince Hamlet. The responses, of the protagonist as well as Gertrude, work to reposition and change the impact of these events. By using *Hamlet*, al-Qaradawi shows the significant juncture created by acts of terror and how they can raise existential questions well beyond the immediate event. Being or not being can indeed mean picking binary sides and refusing to remain neutral during pressing circumstances. As Hamlet asks his mother in her chamber, are you with the usurping king and husband or the rightful one? As al-Qaradawi asks Muslims in this article, are you with a twisted, extremist version of Islam or the authentic one? Making the wrong choice poses an existential risk.

A single and same Shakespearean idea, phrase, or character can be utilised by vastly different people with entirely varied agendas. Indeed, there are endless possibilities when it comes to using Shakespeare as a conduit for one's agenda. Though used to indicate the inevitability of existential threat, such usage rather amusingly proves the complete lack of threat to the lifespan of Shakespeare and his canonical plays! While the previous chapter showed the ways in which Hamlet could be read as a terrorist, this section has indicated how one can, in a way, take whatever they want from Shakespeare. And if Hamlet inspires responses, many of these relate to his thoughts rather than his actions. For terrorists, it is not necessarily about Hamlet's violence, but about ideology, as the Nazis have demonstrated.

STRATFORD'S SWASTIKA

Hamlet can be used as a way of highlighting ideas and ideologies, rather than inspiring violence directly. But ideological justification can just as easily lead to justification of violence. Outside of the English-speaking world, the Germans, with their differing political beliefs, were among the first to respond to Shakespeare. Among these were the Nazis, though German interest in Shakespeare preceded them and was even used as a tool for unification. In 1844, poet Ferdinand Freiligrath summarised the nation's lack of unity and its strive for it by concluding that "Deutschland ist Hamlet".[18] Nonetheless, the Nazis loved the playwright and unsurprisingly, utilised his plays for their own purposes. In fact, over fifty anti-Semitic performances of The Merchant of Venice were put on between 1933 and 1939, twenty in Adolf Hitler's first year as Chancellor. Hitler reportedly described Shylock as "a timelessly valid characterisation of the Jew". A notable production took place in 1943 Byelorussian Minsk "during the liquidation of the last Jewish ghettoes", in which, as Adam Hansen notes, "Shakespeare underwrote, emboldened and consolidated genocide".[19]

This section does not seek to summarise Nazi responses to Shakespeare or consider Nazi appropriations of Shakespeare per se.[20] Rather, by connecting some key aspects of their engagement with Shakespeare, it asks how his works can be used ideologically in order justify some of the most heinous and terrorising violence of the twentieth century. It has already been noted how, as a cultural icon and whether liked or loathed, for a multitude of reasons, it is often worth responding to Shakespeare. References to Shakespeare can, among other things, demonstrate intellect or help explicate an outlook. In Mein Kampf, Hitler used Shakespeare in the same way as many others: "But when nations are fighting for their existence on this earth, when the question of 'to be or not to be' has to be answered, then all humane and aesthetic considerations must be set aside".[21] Rather simply, Hitler utilised Hamlet's question to justify how existential battles can result in inhumane action.

Hitler certainly respected Shakespeare as a cultural icon – he owned his works (the 1925 Georg Müller translation) – and wrote about how Shakespeare was unappreciated in such a degenerate society. In one notepad, Hitler even sketched the scene of Julius Caesar's murder. The Nazis therefore utilised Shakespeare more widely. The concept of *Volksgemeinschaft*, or "people's community", meant that culture needed to be for the good of society not for individual taste. As such, when Shakespeare was performed, the plays had to present Nazi ideals and priorities with clarity, fitting into the *Gleichschaltung* model of totalitarian control and coordination of all aspects of society, including culture. In a degenerate society, as the Nazis would put it, Shakespeare could be used incorrectly. So, for instance, the German Shakespeare Society had to eject its Jewish members and library funding was withheld until it could be proven that there were no Jews remaining.[22] The Reich minister of propaganda, Joseph Goebbels, who had a PhD in dramatic literature and was a published playwright, thought that Shakespeare was "a huge genius" (after watching *Coriolanus* in 1937). The Nazis published a pamphlet titled *Shakespeare: A Germanic Writer* and while at the start, the German dramatist Hans Rothe's translations were being performed, the Germany Shakespeare Society and Goebbels effectively banned them. Instead, they introduced translations that fit *Volksgemeinschaft* and narratives of German supremacy.

More widely, we are reminded of how Shakespeare is used as a statement of culture. When skewed ideologically, this can often present absolutes. That's why for Goebbels there was only one translation of Shakespeare: one that shook off what he saw as the confusing present status of Shakespeare in German and replaced it with a romanticised, simpler ideal. Indeed, ideology can cause simplifications. For terrorists, this might mean a superior or an inferior race, good or evil government, brother or infidel. A simplified version provides an easier message about our own selves. In the 2016 referendum in which the UK voted to leave the European Union, messages about Empire on one hand, and Little England on the other surfaced more than usual. This messaging links closely to ideas about culture. If Shakespeare represents British culture, then Goebbels seems to have appreciated that the German translations in turn are a statement of German culture. Knowing the power that comes with them, statements of culture were exactly what the Nazis sought to control. Spurred by Goebbels and other figures of authority, students across Germany and particularly Berlin ceremoniously burnt books about, among other topics, religion, liberalism, pacifism, and sex. The Nazi regime even burnt books in advance of official publication. Biblioclastic practice has long existed before and after the Nazis. But what we might forget is that what they chose not to burn is as telling as what they did choose to burn. Shakespeare, in this context, becomes more than just words or performances, but rather, a symbol. To me, this context shows Shakespeare's position in extremist regimes: as a valid simplification of cultural statement. One main playwright. One main version of his works. One main interpretation of his works. It is nothing new: in the Bible, Christianity has one main book, and the same can be said of the Qur'an in Islam. For decades in Libya, there was only one book imposed as a life manual, Muammar Gaddafi's The Green Book. It's no surprise that its author is the same dictator who, while praising Shakespeare, told the masses in 1989 that Shakespeare is not British, but that "Sheikh Zubayr" was Arab. He seemed fully serious.[23] And it's perhaps even less surprising that when he was removed from office, piles of his Green Book were publicly burnt.

Ideological utilisation of Shakespeare is significant when coupled with a regime that justifies its own terroristic actions. The next section, then, sheds some light on how Nazi theorist

Carl Schmitt's views on *Hamlet* were used as a justification for extremism, or as Schmitt put it, the right to go against the law.

In performance, *Hamlet* rivalled *The Merchant of Venice* as the most popular play. But rather than the indecisive Hamlet of so many readings, this one was an assertive character who, as one critic put it, is "a Hamlet who knows precisely what he wants".[24] The protagonist played by Gustaf Gründens hundreds of times in Berlin was purposely clear in his intentions, not lamenting the complexity of his situation but using it as a clear drive for revenge; not denying his instincts as Lawrence had viewed him, but as the previous chapter noted, the character can be interpreted as ready for rash action. While such a version was controllable in theatre, this was not the case in schools since teachers could put a different Hamlet forward, one in line with the most common readings. One teacher, Heinrich Hildebrandt, recalls how he was encouraged to teach *The Merchant of Venice* and *Macbeth* and that he taught *A Midsummer Night's Dream*. But the very two plays that most appealed to Hitler, *Julius Caesar* and *Hamlet*, were discouraged in schools. The latter, as he puts it, was "denounced as embodying 'flabbiness of the soul' that the Nazis condemned".[25]

The Nazi education system and propaganda both stemmed from strong ideological beliefs to which readings of Shakespeare almost inevitably contributed. The legal and political theorist Carl Schmitt has been dubbed the "Crown Jurist of the Third Reich". Even as an intellectual whose work has enjoyed a resurgence among political theorists, one must also note Schmitt's active service to and justifications of a terroristic regime: he was certainly a Nazi. In fact, the rather neutral and overly respectful academic treatment of Schmitt is made all the more clear by some banal reproductions of his readings of Shakespeare in social science circles. Indeed, Schmitt's essay *Hamlet or Hecuba: The Intrusion of Time into the Play* (1956) covers his own reading of the play but is also an attempted justification of vividly extremist ideology.

Schmitt places emphasis on the importance of sovereignty, or the freedom of those who are able to proclaim sovereignty. Schmitt asks when one can step outside of the normal, moral parameters of life and citizenship to do things that would normally be unacceptable. Hamlet is going through extreme circumstance and can therefore respond with extreme measures. In other words, when does one have the right to go against the law? To Schmitt, going against the law, including moral or unwritten law, can be justified if there is a state of "exception". He writes, "Sovereign is he who decides the exception".[26] Hamlet eventually decides this exceptional circumstance merits exceptional response. To Schmitt, the Nazis are doing just that given the exceptional circumstances of the war and the alleged threat of Jewish ideas. At that stage, the exception becomes a commendable act: no longer murder but cleansing, not terror but freedom fighting. This is certainly disturbing: how many of us have cheered Hamlet on as he takes revenge into his own hands – as he creates a state of exception in which he has self-formulated the right to go against the law? And we cannot forget that for Schmitt and the Nazis, their actions and culture, their actions and Shakespeare, in some ways go hand in hand. As Fernie implies, the sovereign is "the hero of society", but also the hero of "art". That person, whether a Nazi decision-maker or guard, or indeed a Shakespeare character, no longer has to think within the normal paradigms of their real or dramatic society, but is able to "step beyond good and evil in a terrible (and creative) act".[27]

But I would add that such an act alone is not going to be enough without spectacle. Hamlet's choice not to kill Claudius in the chapel isn't only about damnation: it would be too anonymous and uneventful a vengeance. Like the rather clichéd philosophical question about whether a tree falling in the forest without anyone there to hear it actually makes a sound, is vengeance without anyone noticing worth it for Hamlet? As outlined in the Introduction, terror is above all about symbolism.

In *Richard III*, when the protagonist becomes king, he enters his coronation "in pomp" with trumpets sounding. In earlier quartos, we don't have the trumpets and noblemen accompanying his entrance, nor the detail about him ascending the throne; the additions confirm that we are supposed to notice the magnitude of this spectacle. Richard then begins by asking the question: "But shall we wear these glories for a day? / Or shall they last, and we rejoice in them?" (4.2.6–7). This character knows the power of spectacle and its link to power, and thus seeks for it to be a constant state. It is fascinating that when the real Richard III's skeleton was found under a car park in 2012, a grand procession was arranged for his reburial (some objected due, in large part, to Shakespeare's portrayal, with one tabloid headline reading: "QUEEN TO PAY TRIBUTE TO 'EVIL' KING").[28] The Nazis undoubtedly believed in the power of spectacle as a way of cementing an aesthetic and cultural identity. They utilised processions, banners, and flags regularly, appropriating the style of Imperial Rome. Even the Mercedes-Benz car built for Hitler was symbolic. Most famously, the Nuremberg Rally masterminded the idea of a curated spectacle, orchestrating the visual politics and style of Nazism: powerful, historical, organised, and grand.

Both for terrorists and on the Shakespearean stage, blood is one of the clearest symbols. Around half of the 150-plus deaths that happen across the plays are from stabbings. The majority of deaths in, for instance, *Romeo and Juliet*, *Hamlet*, *Othello*, *Macbeth*, and *Julius Caesar* are from stabbings and beheadings. The exceptions tend to be women: Lady Montague (heart-ache), Gertrude (poison), Ophelia (drowning), Desdemona (smothered with a pillow), Portia (eating hot coals), and Cleopatra (snakebite). The display of Ophelia's body in the water and Cleopatra's ultimate suicide suggest that these deaths are arguably even more dramatic than the stabbings. Nonetheless, the majority of deaths and some of the most important in the canon are rife with blood, including in the most violent play, *Titus Andronicus*. The Royal Shakespeare Company (RSC) production of *Titus Andronicus* in 2017 is said to have seen at least one person leave in shock mid-performance during every single show. When the RSC tested audience reactions using heart rate monitors, watching the play was the equivalent of a five-minute cardiovascular workout. But shock levels were lower for those watching in cinemas compared to theatres, suggesting that we are more desensitised to violence on the screen.[29] The following year's production of John Webster's *The Duchess of Malfi* was also particularly bloody, so much so that sheets were handed out to the front rows.

The term "blood" appears almost 1,000 times in Shakespeare's canon (including 689 times as "blood" or "bloods" and 234 as "bloody"). Of course, blood can be very symbolic in general and can link to violence, family ties, menstruation, and more. There is something to be said about its symbolism at war and related to death. Giving one's blood for a nation or cause, for instance, has been perceived over different eras as a commendable thing. But many also see that blood has a different price depending on whose it is and which side of a border they live on. It is about more, no doubt, than just violence.

One could argue that Shakespeare's audiences have always been excited by violence – and that it is by no means exclusive to his plays or theatre. But the power of visual violence is significant in triggering feelings. Terror groups use such visuals, uploading gory videos – nowadays professionally edited – so that they can create shock (or for a twisted few, inspiration). It has also been proven that when terror attacks occur, many people gravitate towards the violent videos of the incident. The most telling event in recent times was the 2013 terror incident in Woolwich, London. A British soldier, Lee Rigby, was murdered by two men who ran him over with a car before stabbing him with a knife and hacking him with a cleaver. The symbolism of the attack was clear. This was a soldier innocently going about his day and after his murder, they dragged him into the road and engaged with the public. They had done this to avenge Muslims being killed by the British Army, they claimed, talking to passers-by and even handing them a handwritten note about what they had done.

Most shockingly, one of the killers, Michael Adebolajo, spoke directly into a passer-by's phone camera:

I apologise that women had to witness this today but in our lands women have to see the same. You people will never be safe. Remove your governments, they don't care about you. You think David Cameron is gonna get caught in the street when we start busting our guns? Do you think politicians are going to die? No, it's going to be the average guy, like you and your children. So get rid of them. Tell them to bring our troops back.[30]

Not only was this attacker attempting to justify his actions, he was also confirming their symbolism. The distressing power of the symbolism has led to copy-cat attempts, with at least two men imprisoned for attempting to emulate the event. A man named Zack Davies, a neo-Nazi member of a far-right group, was given a life sentence in 2015 for attacking a Sikh man in similar fashion with a machete, shouting "white power" as he did so and citing revenge for Rigby's murder as his motive.[31] What's more, that Adebolajo confirmed the intentions of his actions on video further ensures the spectacle of the event. But most chillingly, during the immediate aftermath of the murder (the fourteen or so minutes before armed police arrived to shoot the pair), the attacker's hands were drenched in blood, completely red: the first image anyone will recollect from this terrible incident. Those hands looked un-washable, reminiscent of the most famous images in Macbeth. When Macbeth sees his bloodied hands, he laments the "sorry sight" (2.2.25):

Will all great Neptune's ocean wash this blood
Clean from my hands? No, this my hand will rather
The multitudinous seas incarnadine,
Making the green one red.

(2.2.71–74)

Lady Macbeth complains that "the smell of blood still" lurks; even "[a]ll the perfumes of Arabia will not sweeten this little hand" (5.1.37–38).

***

Through today, Shakespeare's hometown of Stratford-upon-Avon celebrates his birthday every April. Following the eighteenth-century actor David Garrick's Stratford Jubilee of 1769, celebrating Shakespeare became an annual and public undertaking. According to Michael Dobson, it "marked the instigation of Bardolatry, of the Stratford-upon-Avon tourist industry, of Shakespeare's central place in national and international public culture".[32] While it is true that it had an impact on the UK and undoubtedly on Stratford-upon-Avon, it is hardly the case that Shakespeare's place in "international public culture" was instigated by the Jubilee. Rather, it was affected variously by colonisation before that and cultural or social events within those particular locales after that. Nonetheless (and despite heavy rain on its second day), the Jubilee helped to put Shakespeare's birthplace on the map and the birthday celebrations have continued since.

As part of these celebrations, states are invited to unfurl and fly their flags in Stratford-upon-Avon. During and after wartime, states that were regarded as enemies were excluded from these invitations. Germany was excluded for ten years after World War One and seven after the World War Two (alongside Japan). But in April 1939, less than five months before Germany invaded Poland, a swastika flag flew over Stratford-upon-Avon, just a few hundred feet from Shakespeare's birthplace (Figure 3.1). In her study of the international collections of the birthplace, Helen Hopkins indicates that the inclusion of this flag could have been "a sign of diplomacy that supported the appeasement efforts to avoid another war".[33] Hopkins also hints that the local press appeared to be sceptical of the Axis alliance flags in their reports; the *Stratford Herald* notes excitedly that "the German Charge d'Affaires pulled the wrong cord and brought his country's emblem tumbling to the ground in a

Figure 3.1 Shakespeare's birthday celebrations: Nazi Flag on Bridge Street, by Arthur Locke, 1939 (© Shakespeare Birthplace Trust).

bundle" while "the Japanese flag refused to fly".[34] Nonetheless, this does not negate the fact that a swastika flew over Stratford to celebrate Shakespeare's birthday.

The Nazis would of course go on to use Shakespeare for their own purposes, though this is also a reminder that their appropriation of Shakespeare is nowhere near as fatal as their appropriation of the swastika. For hundreds of years, the swastika was used in the religious traditions of India (in Hinduism, Jainism, and Buddhism) as a symbol of divinity, spirituality, and prosperity, until it was turned into a hateful symbol of extremist Aryan identity. In *Mein Kampf*, Hitler claims to have designed the flag himself and the swastika became the most recognisable sign of Nazi propaganda, including in their rallies.

Returning to the 1939 swastika flag, the incident should not be treated in isolation. Utilisation of Shakespeare is by no means fixed to one perspective of political history. The Shakespearean actor Antony Sher, a South African Jew (and Prince Charles' favourite actor), protested against the South Africa flag in birthday celebrations during the apartheid. In 1987, the organising committee decided not to invite South Africa's representatives, something which caused displeasure among the establishment. At the time, critic Philip Brockbank complained that it "transformed a once inconsequential and delightful festival into a local as well as a national political forum".[35]

These flags are all a reminder that Shakespeare's position and legacy, and the power associated with these, is far from straightforward. Does using Shakespeare for diplomacy confirm his position as a British symbol, of the establishment in particular (therefore linked to the West, colonisation, and war), and in turn shed further light on why some terrorists have loathed what he represents? Or is it that the soft power associated with Shakespeare's life and works can appeal to different factions? From those who mean well to those who want to terrorise, from those who want to utilise Shakespeare, whether by appropriating or by attacking, this has a lot to do with power.

That Shakespeare and (often soft) power are so integrally linked is a further manifestation of the importance of spectacle and symbolism. Visiting Shakespeare's birthplace today, as hundreds have done over the years (including Bin Laden), one is met with security guards who search your bags before allowing entrance. In reality, searches like these, like frisking (pat-downs) outside sports stadia, take little more than a few seconds. Their primary aim is to act as a deterrent, one that is only possible through the power of spectacle. It also serves as a symbol of fear for any potential perpetrators and safety for the very vast majority. Like and within propaganda, spectacle is particularly important as a show of power and as a message against terror. It's one of the reasons that soldiers have military funerals; in Rigby's case, a well-attended (including Prime Minister Cameron) and well-reported memorial was essential to the power and symbolism of the counter-narrative. And armies worldwide put huge emphasis on spectacle. A friend serving as a Sergeant in the Egyptian Army in the early 2010s told me about the time his superiors greeted news of a high-profile inspection with long days in which everyone had to paint the army vehicles in fresh khaki. When the inspectors arrived, everything was in tiptop condition as they glided past in just seconds after weeks of preparation. They were satisfied, but little did they know that these impeccable looking, perfectly lined vehicles didn't even have engines in them!

EPILOGUE: THE ANARCHIC STATUS QUO

The events highlighted – whether real (like the Danish cartoon controversy, the assassination of Foda, and the Nazi propaganda performances) or fictional (like the injustices and viciousness in Hamlet, The Merchant of Venice, Richard III, and Titus Andronicus) – have something in common. They manifest conscious decisions to go against what may be perceived as a common moral code or law. The result is anarchy. Rather than anarchy in which there is no centralised power, the anarchy presented here represents a non-recognition of moral law. Aristotle and Plato believed that "human beings flourished within just political communities", while modern political philosophy identifies "obedience to the law" and more importantly "the ideal of a rule of law" as "noble and enlightened".[36] In liberal political philosophy today, this obedience is simply assumed.

It is important to note that terrorist and extremist actions and justifications, and even simply violence against others, are propagations of anarchy since they go against the status quo. But that status quo is upheld by law and where that system is not able to stand on its own feet, trouble begins. Hamlet has lost faith in the system, Richard III is trying to overhaul the system, Shylock is not protected by the system. The law may well manifest order, but it can also benefit particular individuals or groups at the expense of others. Is it really that big a surprise that Shylock, let down by the system and abused, resorts to threats of violence? He only desires Antonio's flesh for that reason: "If it will feed nothing else, it will feed my revenge" (3.1.37). This is Shylock's spectacle: as a mistreated second-class citizen he wants to take things into his own hands and to perform some sort of power, albeit in the wrong manner.

Anarchy, then, is more likely to take place when identity is not captured within the beneficiaries of the society and law. And so we return once more to the question of identity. When it comes down to it, who is protected by the system? For instance, can one blame a young black man for feeling that, were he to go through the judicial system, it would not protect him? For extremists this means taking things into their own hands with devastating consequences for everyone. And by using *Hamlet* to explain the state of exception and the right to go against the law, Schmitt understood the power of this message very well.

In the case of the Nazis, the lines are more convoluted because they were the actual state. Philosopher Giorgio Agamben has advanced understanding of Schmitt's state of exception by tracing it to the Roman *justitium*, essentially their state of emergency. Agamben notes that at times of crises like terrorist attacks or threats, the state of emergency is essentially the same as the state of exception since constitutional rights are not necessarily upheld.[37] Depending on the country, this includes broader search warrants, increased time holding suspects without charge, as well as questions about rights to citizenship and rights during imprisonment (most famously, Guantanamo Bay). Brad Evans has written about this in *Liberal Terror*, which critiques the "liberal terror" upheld through global security and what Michel Foucault named *le biopouvoir*, or biopower (political power revolving around the population rather than the individual). For Evans, the global security model advanced by counter-terror narratives legitimises liberalism's governance on our lives, so much so that the increased securitisation results, perhaps ironically, in a constant feeling of being under threat: everything becomes terrorising.[38]

Can we, then, consider terrorism as a constructed point of view, as an abstraction rather than a material fact? Have our ideological battle lines become so blurred compared to wartime, for instance, that we require a common enemy? While one wouldn't want to deconstruct a real threat as insubstantial, there is little doubt that state propaganda is a part of the terrorism narrative. This does not have to be a call to arms. It can be an emphasis of vigilance. Or it can be the way the enemy is presented. One such example was the media's emphasis on Bin Laden's significant pornographic stash, as though it is that which will make us realise his immoral nature. For those working in counter-terror, that particular fact was not a surprise: terrorists have had a relationship with pornography for decades (for example, ISIS beheading videos are shot in similar fashion to pornography and the group has even helped distribute pornography).[39]

Shakespeare does, in some ways, imply an understanding of the role of the state. Through this understanding, he was able to become part of the establishment, writing plays that the royals would enjoy and relishing a celebrity status. We might even note, rather tongue in cheek, that his writings were never burnt despite this being a common activity at times of Tudor and Stuart rule.[40] But this understanding also fed into his plots and characters. It's one of the key reasons he emphasises the importance of propaganda in *Henry V*, the power of rhetoric in *Julius Caesar*, the complexity of political allegiances in *Antony and Cleopatra*, and the ways in which a state and its head can try to reach a status in which they become unquestionable and unaccountable, like in *Richard III*. It's also why the plots of *Macbeth* and *Cymbeline* navigate complex contexts of succession and its relation to British identity. In all of these plays, the state is obviously able to define and influence identity.

On the other hand, Shakespeare also presents the plight of second-class citizens like the lower classes in *Henry VI, Part 2* and Shylock in *The Merchant of Venice*. In the latter, Shylock will "impeach the freedom of the state, / If they deny him justice" (3.2.284–85). Antonio admits that Venice will uphold the free trading laws it relies on, because if they do not, its leaders, including the Duke, will lose credibility: "if it be denied, / Will much impeach the justice of the state" (3.3.31–32). Here, Shakespeare shows awareness of the state's sensitive position as it negotiates its activities on the basis of economic interest, not just ideology. It is an important reminder: any war – the War on Terror included – is at its core linked to economic interests, be it related to gaining land, weakening a rival, or trading arms, oil, or opium. In the end, the status quo is at best inevitably open for anarchic response and at worst anarchic in and of itself. That way, ideology and power can be performed through spectacular displays – or in some cases, through appropriation and quotation.

NOTES

1 D. H. Lawrence, *Twilight in Italy*, in *D. H. Lawrence and Italy* (New York: Penguin, 1985), 68.

2 D. H. Lawrence, "Why I Don't Like Living in London", in *Late Essays and Article*, ed. James T. Boulton (Cambridge: Cambridge University Press, 2004), 120–22 (120). Lawrence explores violence widely in such works as *The Prussian Officer* and *Women in Love*. I am grateful to Gemma Moss for her insight on Lawrence.

3 Patrick Kingsley, *How to Be Danish: A Journey to the Cultural Heart of Denmark* (London: Short Books, 2012), 97–100.

4 "Arrest Extremist Marchers, Police Told", *The Guardian* (6 February 2006), www.theguardian.com/uk/2006/feb/06/raceandreligion. muhammadcartoons [accessed 4 June 2020].

5 "Arla Cheesed Off over Middle East Boycott", *The Daily Telegraph* (4 February 2006), www.telegraph.co.uk/finance/2931522/Arla-cheesed-off-over-Middle-East-boycott.html [accessed 23 July 2020].

6 Cinnamon Stillwell, "Something Is Rotten Outside the State of Denmark" (8 February 2006), www.sfgate.com/politics/article/Something-Is-Rotten-Outside-the-State-of-Denmark-2522905.php [accessed 23 July 2020]. Emphasis in title added.

7   Shari Forbes, Soren Blau and Sasha Voss, "Deadly Secrets – The Science of Decomposition", *Australian Academy of Science* (2016), www.science. org.au/curious/decomposition [accessed 6 January 2021]; Priyanka Boghani, "Syria Massacre: UN Observers Greeted by Smell of Burnt Flesh", *The World* (8 June 2012), www.pri.org/stories/2012-06-08/ syria-massacre-un-observers-greeted-smell-burnt-flesh [both accessed 6 January 2021].

8   Mya Guarnieri, "Unruly Building Enguls East Jerusalem Life", *Al Jazeera English* (4 May 2013), www.aljazeera.com/features/2013/5/4/ unruly-building-engulfs-east-jerusalem-life [accessed 6 January 2021].

9   Matthew Moore, "Half of Councils Use Anti-Terror Laws to Spy on 'Bin Crimes'", *Daily Telegraph* (1 November 2008), www.telegraph. co.uk/news/uknews/3333366/Half-of-councils-use-anti-terror-laws-to-spy-on-bin-crimes.html [accessed 6 January 2021]; Ben Messenger, "Middlesbrough Council Removes Risk of Waste Collection Vehicles Being Stole & Used in Terror Attacks", *Waste Management World* (27 September 2017), https://waste-management-world.com/a/ middlesbrough-council-removes-risk-of-waste-collection-vehicles-being-stole-used-in-terror-attacks [accessed 6 January 2021].

10 In fact, Shakespeare links terror to smell in *Macbeth* – via the smell of gunpowder. See Jonathan Gil Harris, "The Smell of Gunpowder: *Macbeth* and the Palimpsests of Olfaction", in *Untimely Matter in the Time of Shakespeare* (Philadelphia: University of Pennsylvania Press, 2009), 119–40.

11 Margaret Litvin, *Hamlet's Arab Journey: Shakespeare's Prince and Nasser's Ghost* (Princeton: Princeton University Press, 2011), 18. See Litvin's chapter "Hamlet in the Daily Discourse" for many fascinating examples of "To be, or not to be" in the region. There are many more, too; far too many to list.

12 Farag Foda, *Nakūn aw lā Nakūn* (Alexandria: al-Mustaqbal, 1988), 6–7.

13 Ashraf Abdel-Hamid, "Egyptian Extremist Abu el-Alaa Abdrabu Confirmed Killed in Syria Air Strike", *Al Arabiya News* (23 March 2017), https://english.alarabiya.net/en/News/middle-east/2017/03/23/ Egyptian-extremist-Abu-el-Alaa-Abdrabu-confirmed-killed-in-Syria-air-strike [accessed 12 August 2020].

14 "Gaddafi's Plot to Assassinate 'Colonel' Adel Imam", *Albawaba* (23 September 2016), www.albawaba.com/entertainment/gaddafis-plot-assassinate-colonel-adel-imam-885296 [accessed 6 January 2021].

15 "Egyptian Actor Adel Imam Wins Appeal in Defaming Islam Case", *Ahram Online* (12 September 2012), http://english.ahram.org.eg/NewsContent/1/64/52683/Egypt/Politics-/Egyptian-actor-Adel-Imam-wins-appeal-in-defaming-I.aspx [accessed 6 January 2021].

16 Litvin, *Hamlet's Arab Journey*, 23. Litvin is correct to note that the phrase represents "an already understood moral imperative", but in disassociating it from Shakespeare, Litvin risks overlooking the nature of Arafat's rhetorical (literary) style, and second, that the subsequent reception, not just the initial utterance, confirm that the association with Shakespeare remains robust even when secondary.

17 Yusuf al-Qaradawi, "Al-Hiwār bayn al-Islām wal-Naṣrāniyyah" [Dialogue between Islam and Christianity], *Al-Hiwar Today* (29 December 2001), www.alhiwartoday.net/node/7279 [accessed 13 August 2020]. First discussed in Litvin, 21–22. Litvin mistakenly reads "*maʿnā wa jadwā*" (meaning and feasibility) as "*maʿnā wujūdi*" (existential meaning).

18 Andrew Dickson, *Worlds Elsewhere: Journeys around Shakespeare's Globe* (London: Bodley Head), 45.

19 Andrew G. Bonnell, *Shylock in Germany: Antisemitism and the German Theatre from the Enlightenment to the Nazis* (London: Tauris Academic Studies, 2008), 141; Adam Hansen, "Shakespeare and Extremism", *Critical Survey* 30.4 (2018): 95–113, 103.

20 On this topic, see Rodney Symington, *The Nazi Appropriation of Shakespeare: Cultural Politics in the Third Reich* (Lewiston: Mellen, 2005); Andreas Höfele, *No Hamlets: German Shakespeare from Nietzsche to Carl Schmitt* (Oxford: Oxford University Press, 2016).

21 Adolf Hitler, *Mein Kampf* (Mumbai, Jaico, 2018), 168.

22 Ruth Freifrau von Ledebur, "'The Country That Gave Birth to You a Second Time': An Essay about the Political History of the German Shakespeare Society 1918–1945", in *German Shakepeare Studies at the Turn of the Century*, ed. Christa Jansohn (Newark: Delaware University Press, 2006), 255–71, 265–66.

23 Ferial Ghazoul notes that this Arab name for Shakespeare "started in the late nineteenth century with the Lebanese writer Ahmad Faris

Al-Shidyaq (1804–88)". See Ferial Ghazoul, "The Arabization of *Othello*", *Comparative Literature* 50.1 (Winter 1998): 1–31, 9. It is worth noting that al-Shidyaq wrote satires and was famed for his wordplay. This confirms that Gaddafi, like some other Arabs, was missing the joke.

24 Dickson, *Worlds Elsewhere*, 76.

25 Milton Mayer, *They Thought They Were Free: The Germans, 1933–45* (London: University of Chicago Press, 2013), 193.

26 Carl Schmitt, *Political Theology: Four Chapters on the Concept of Sovereignty*, ed. and trans. George Schwab (Chicago: University of Chicago Press, 2005), 6.

27 Fernie, in Issa, "Shakespeare and Terrorism", *BBC Radio 3*, unpublished recording

28 Front page of the *Sunday Express* on 21 March 2015. Another tabloid, a columnist anguished, "with mounting stupefaction" that "the world had gone stark staring bonkers" as it watched the "grotesque televised travesty" of "without question one of the most evil, detestable tyrants ever to walk this earth". See Michael Thornton, "It's Mad to Make This Child Killer a National Hero: Richard III Was One of the Most Evil, Detestable Tyrants Ever to Walk This Earth", *Daily Mail* (24 March 2015), www.dailymail.co.uk/debate/article-3008671/Richard-III-one-evil-detestable-tyrants-walk-earth.html [accessed 7 November 2019].

29 "Shakespeare Still Has Power to Shock – RSC *Titus Andronicus* Audience Research Project Results", *Royal Shakespeare Company* (2017), www.rsc.org.uk/press/releases/shakespeare-still-has-power-to-shock---rsc-titus-andronicus-audience-research-project-results [accessed 7 January 2021].

30 "Woolwich Attack: The Terrorist's Rant", *Daily Telegraph* (23 May 2013), www.telegraph.co.uk/news/uknews/terrorism-in-the-uk/10075488/Woolwich-attack-the-terrorists-rant.html [accessed 7 January 2021].

31 BBC News, "Lee Rigby Revenge Attacker Zack Davies Given Life Sentence", *BBC News* (11 September 2015), www.bbc.co.uk/news/uk-wales-north-east-wales-34218184 [accessed 8 January 2021].

32 Michael Dobson, "Reviving Garrick", in *New Places: Shakespeare and Civic Creativity*, ed. Paul Edmondson and Ewan Fernie (London: Arden, 2018), 3–22, 4.

33 Helen Hopkins, "'Gifts of the World'?: Creating and Contextualizing the Shakespeare Birthplace Trust's International Collections", PhD diss. (Birmingham City University, 2021).

34 Ibid.; Susan Brock and Sylvia Morris, "'Enchanted Ground': Celebrating Shakespeare's Birthday in Stratford-upon-Avon", in *Shakespeare Jubilees: 1769–2014*, ed. Christa Jansohn and Dieter Mehl (Zurich: Lit Verlag, 2015), 31–56, 47.

35 Philip Brockbank, "Shakespeare's Stratford and South Africa", *Shakespeare Quarterly* 38.4 (1987): 479–81, 479; see Barbara Hodgdon, *The Shakespeare Trade: Performances and Appropriations* (Philadelphia: University of Pennsylvania Press, 1998), 248.

36 Andrew Fiala, "Anarchism", *The Stanford Encyclopedia of Philosophy*, ed. Edward N. Zalta (Spring 2018), https://plato.stanford.edu/archives/spr2018/entries/anarchism/ [accessed 14 January 2021].

37 Giorgio Agamben, *State of Exception*, trans. Kevin Attell (London: University of Chicago Press, 2015).

38 Brad Evans, *Liberal Terror* (Cambridge: Polity, 2013).

39 Simon Cottee, "The Pornography of Jihadism: What ISIS Videos and X-Rated Movies Have in Common", *The Atlantic* (12 September 2014), www.theatlantic.com/international/archive/2014/09/isis-jihadist-propaganda-videos-porn/380117/ [accessed 14 January 2021].

40 David Cressy, "Book Burning in Tudor and Stuart England", *The Sixteenth Century Journal* 36.2 (Summer 2005): 359–74.

Identity and assassination

Four

DIPLOMATIC SHAKESPEARE

The swastika flag is not the only one to have caused controversy in Stratford-upon-Avon. The Confederate flag – used by Southern states in the American Civil War (1861–1865) and now widely regarded as a symbol of white supremacy and slavery – has been spotted repeatedly outside the US. The flag represents the (seven, then eleven) Confederate States of America, who in 1861 separated from the US after Abraham Lincoln's election victory the previous year. Lincoln's antislavery stance concerned the Southern enslavers and led to a four-year Civil War that defeated the Confederacy and propelled the abolishment of slavery through the 13th Amendment. It would also be a factor in the Lincoln's assassination, to which we shall return.

In summer 2017, a number of Confederate flags were flown in Stratford-upon-Avon. Specifically, it was put up at a caravan heritage rally on the town's racecourse.[1] With a walking path nearby, the flag was spotted by two separate US citizens living in Stratford-upon-Avon, both of whom happen to be Shakespeare scholars, namely Katie Brokaw and Karen Harker (then a graduate student). Harker ventured to the fairground with flyers to explain the origins of the flag but after some hostile responses was advised by security to leave. Responses

159 **Identity and assassination**

DOI: 10.4324/9780429320088-5

from Brokaw, Harker, and a third US Shakespeare scholar in Stratford, Erin Sullivan, varied from contact to the Council, to the local *Stratford Herald* newspaper (who did not want to run a story), to the owners of the field, and to the group responsible for the flag. Sullivan and Brokaw talked directly to the group responsible via social media, with Brokaw explaining the history of the flag and "what was unfolding" at that same time "in Charlottesville (where the Confederate and Nazi flags flew side by side)".[2]

Indeed, in June 2015, a twenty-one year-old white supremacist named Dylann Roof attacked the Mother Emanuel Church, home to one of the oldest black congregations in the south, in what would be known as the Charleston church massacre, one of the most fatal attacks on a place of worship in modern US history. Nine African-Americans were killed and Roof was sentenced to death. This event affected the status of the Confederate flag directly. Many flags flew at half-staff after this shooting. Since South Carolina law prohibited flag alterations without a legislative vote, the Confederate flag above the state's Confederate Monument was not lowered. Protests began and high-profile figures like President Barack Obama began to join the debate, while retailers stopped selling it. By July, the state Senate voted to remove the flag. In response, the Unite the Right Rally in August 2017 saw hundreds of white supremacists, including alt-right, neo-Nazi, and Ku Klux Klan members protest against the removal of Confederate monuments and flags, including the statue of Confederate General Robert E. Lee. Then, another terrorist attack took place. James Alex Fields Jr., who had neo-Nazi beliefs, drove his car into a group of counter-protesters, killing one and injuring nine. In response, the City Council voted to remove the statue and when this was blocked by state law, the statue was shrouded in black.

Back in Stratford-upon-Avon, in response to the enquiries and criticisms, the campers responsible for the flag, from the Redditch Westerners Association, argued that for them this was an act of historical remembrance, not a political statement. They had run their annual Blue Rodeo for a number of years without issue and as self-defined Western enthusiasts appear to have been reenacting an imagined version of US history based on their favourite movies (especially noting the name Westerners not Southerners). In the end, while organisers agreed that the Confederate flag and Southern cross would not be displayed on any event infrastructure like the stage, they would not stop anyone from wearing it on costumes or flying it on tents and caravans.

While the Stratford District Council seems to have responded judiciously in general, there are a number of side issues that seemed to affect this event. First, that the government body did not want to appear to be censoring or regulating per se. Second, the timing coincided with the contexts related to terror attacks in the actual Southern States (where the majority of the Redditch Westerners Association members had probably never been). These events were taking place at the exact same time that the Confederate flag was spotted in Stratford-upon-Avon, meaning the Council had to respond and that the flag was, regardless of any claim to the contrary, a political statement. The third issue that affected this flag is Shakespeare. People around the world relate the town to the playwright and much of its reputation and economy is related to, if not built around, its most famous resident. Another small market town would have much less at stake, many less international visitors, and much less media attention. Did the Council review take this into consideration? The Council's Licensing Officer notes that a locale's reputation or history cannot lawfully be used as the basis for its licensing decisions. That being said, the review of this licence does seem to consider, even informally or unconsciously, Stratford's international standing and the concurrent events in Charlottesville. The town's standing is vital and has economic implications (for example, the Shakespeare Birthplace Trust and Royal Shakespeare Theatre attract tourists, professionals, and students who contribute to the town's healthy hotel and restaurant industry). Would there be less urgency to question the flag were it not in Shakespeare's town? Legally, Shakespeare does not influence the town regulation. But it is rather inevitable that the review can be read as: how do we deal with the Confederate flag in *Shakespeare's* Stratford? The spectacle and symbolism go both ways. The Confederate flag has its own symbolism and is used for its own spectacle. And Shakespeare (in the form of his legacy and birth town) also has a public-facing image associated to him: where possible he has to be kept away, symbolically, from things that risk putting him on the wrong side of history.

The Confederate link to Shakespeare's birth town existed long before these events. Rather strangely, the Shakespeare Birthplace Trust owns a walking stick belonging to the Confederate President Jefferson Davis. The stick has a photograph and catalogue entry in the Birthplace Trust's collections, but equally strange is the fact that it has gone missing.[3] Minutes away from the birthplace stands Harvard House (managed by the Shakespeare Birthplace Trust since 1990), built in 1596 by Thomas Rogers, grandfather of Harvard University's benefactor, John Harvard. In 1909, it was purchased and renovated by Edward Morris of Chicago at the suggestion of British novelist Marie Corelli who had moved to Stratford. Helen Hopkins explains:

> Corelli's father, Dr. Charles Mackay, had met and befriended
> Davis in Richmond, Virginia, where he was working as a
> correspondent on the US Civil War ... Davis was imprisoned
> for two years after the war then embarked on a tour of
> Europe, meeting Mackay in Scotland in 1869, where they
> went on a walking tour together. Their friendly exchange of
> walking sticks at their parting led to the stick being passed
> to Marie Corelli, who left it to the Harvard House collection
> in her will.[4]

It is also worth mentioning that Warwickshire became a hub
for Confederates in the immediate aftermath of the Civil War.
Specifically, the town of Leamington Spa, around ten miles
north of Stratford-upon-Avon, saw a nest of Confederates take
refuge there. The region sympathised with their cause and
was perfectly positioned with rail connections to Stratford,
London, and Liverpool (the latter city a key supporter of the
Confederates and the slave trade).

The previous chapters have shown varied responses to and
readings of Shakespeare's works and characters. There are
terrorists and extremists who disliked Shakespeare and there
are those who were inspired by their readings of his plots
and characters ideologically. And then there are those who are
not only inspired but carry out their violence directly. These
include the Confederate spy and Shakespearean actor John
Wilkes Booth who, in April 1865, assassinated Lincoln.

OPPOSITIONAL FREEDOMS

Since 1872, Central Park, New York, has boasted an impres-
sive bronze sculpture of Shakespeare. The statue was made
possible thanks in large part to funding from ticket sales

to the performance of Julius *Caesar* at the Winter Garden Theatre in November 1864, equivalent to over $100,000 in today's money.

The nineteenth-century actor Junius Brutus Booth was a leading Shakespeare actor. He fled England (and his wife) to the US when his mistress became pregnant. His illegitimate sons included Edwin Booth (the most renowned Shakespeare actor of his time in the US, even giving performances to Lincoln) and the now well-known John Wilkes Booth. It is well documented that Junius picked the more talented son, Edwin, to go on tour with him while John Wilkes remained in boarding school. When Junius' wife came to take her share of the fortune and left the Booths less stable financially, Junius and Edwin ventured to California to make money. Some analyses claim that John Wilkes had an outcast profile: an illegitimate child feeling undervalued by his father and with a sibling rivalry that extended further when Edwin, having become a celebrity actor, prevented John Wilkes from joining him. That is, until this performance of Julius *Caesar*. Alongside a third brother, Junius Jr., they put on a hugely anticipated play in order to raise money for the Central Park statue. Edwin played Brutus while John Wilkes played Mark Antony (Figure 4.1).

Historian Nora Titone writes: "At the moment the second act began, the doors leading into the auditorium burst open and firefighters poured into the theater … The audience leaped out of their seats, ready to run for an exit".[5] Though the theatre was fine and the performance continued after the place was checked, this interruption, like in Qatar, was the consequence of a terrorist attack. A network of Confederates – the Confederate Army of Manhattan – had attempted to burn New York City to the ground by starting simultaneous fires at over twenty major buildings, most of them hotels (including

Figure 4.1 John Wilkes Booth, Edwin Booth, and Junius Booth, Jr. (from left to right) in Shakespeare's *Julius Caesar* in 1864.

one next door to the theatre). The plan failed. Discussing the event with his brothers, John Wilkes is said to have legitimised the actions of that night and sympathised with what he called an "act of war", resulting in eviction from his brother's house.[6] John Wilkes had cemented these beliefs over years, including in Baltimore where he joined the Knights of the Golden Circle, a pro-Confederate society that sought to create a new government in which slavery was actively encouraged. It was also in Baltimore where, playing Macbeth, he is said to have had a signature move: a fifteen foot jump, "plummeting to the stage from a precipice" the first time he meets the witches.[7]

Around five months after *Julius Caesar*, as is well known, John Wilkes Booth became the first person to assassinate a US president, shooting Lincoln at Ford's Theatre in Washington DC during a performance of *Our American Cousin*. He is thought to have used his signature Macbeth jump to land where he wished in the presidential box. After shooting Lincoln at close range from behind, he is said to have uttered that same word hovering through this book: "Freedom". More famously, witness accounts suggest he then shouted "*sic semper tyrannis*" (thus always to tyrants), which shares parallels with perceptions of Julius Caesar's assassination. Some accounts note that as Booth escaped, a spur caught the bunting and tripped him up, possibly fracturing his leg. The spurs also had a Shakespearean link: they were part of his father's costume for *Richard III*.

Ironically, five days before the assassination, Lincoln celebrated the end of the Civil War with friends by reading a passage from *Macbeth*: the moments after Macbeth assassinates King Duncan and is in a state of moral confusion. Days later, Lincoln would be in Duncan's position and Booth would be in Macbeth's, though confused about how to stay on the run, not the moral implications of his actions. Booth even ended an explanatory letter with Macbeth's "I must fight the course" (5.7.2).

The majority of these events are well known. But in the context of this discussion, it is worth reflecting on a number of issues. Take the choice of location for the assassination. Most obviously, people knew who Booth was here, so he was able to enter the theatre. He had performed here before, so knew his way around the theatre well. He knew the habits of the audience so could pick the right time to enter. He knew the play by heart so picked a moment when there would be loud laughter. Second, for Booth, the symbolism of the theatre was significant. Titone argues that his rivalry with his brother had a significant effect on this event. Choosing the theatre may confirm this: he could finally upstage his brother in the theatre. Third, the fact is that we come to expect violence and action in the theatre. A play is such because it involves both language and action. Shakespeare as language alone remains incomplete and as action alone remains incomplete. Booth's terroristic interjection is an action embedded within the action of the play on show. It was even mistaken by audience members to be part of the performance. After all, theatre is a place where extraordinary and unexpected things – including unimaginable violence and ordinarily absurd metatheatricalities – can be expected quite ordinarily.

The wider concern is that Shakespeare's work is vast – and in the wrong hands, it can radicalise. As Fernie has argued, "we are excited" by the most morally wicked characters and can "feel the more alive for it".[8] No matter how familiar we might be with the incident and its afterlife, Booth's emulation of his favourite characters is nothing short of a case in point. As an avid Shakespeare fan and actor, heavily influenced by the murder of the ruler in *Julius Caesar* and *Macbeth*, his actions point to interpretations of two concepts: freedom and truth.

In the case of Booth and Lincoln, competing perceptions of freedom come into play again. At a basic level, on one hand, freedom of the south (Booth); on another, freedom of the slave (Lincoln).[9] To recall the second chapter's epilogue, even Lincoln's version could be regarded as incomplete since "freedom from" needs to be coupled with a "freedom to"; the latter was not provided to slaves in the aftermath of emancipation, with former slaves left on the streets unable to find employment and healthcare. Even if, as some would have it, the Confederates were not fighting for slavery, their fight for sovereignty included the question of abolition and their answer to it was clear enough. It is curious that Booth, writing to his mother, describes himself as living like "a slave in the north". Like many terrorists, like Hamlet, Booth's freedom paradox included the freedom of the South based on a lack of freedom for others: in this case, an inhumane un-freedom.

Furthermore, Booth became obsessed with the idea of tyranny and specifically that Lincoln is a tyrant. He internalised this into an expected truth, much as in Shakespeare's tragedies, we might expect a tyrannical antagonist. Indeed, when we recall that Booth saw himself as cast in the Shakespearean mould, this is not an allusion to characters alone, but to the world around those characters: one in which, among other things, language must be accompanied by action. By committing his act, as well as becoming the most famous Booth, he expected to become a hero, much like his self-confessed favourite character Brutus by the end of *Julius Caesar*, remembered in the final scene as "the noblest Roman of them all" (5.5.73). There is a side of the argument that suggests it worked: the poem "Our Brutus" was set to music and could be heard in the south into the 1890s.[10] What Booth did succeed in is attaching his name to one of the most famous recorded assassinations in history: almost as famous, perhaps, as that of Julius Caesar.

The key difference between *Julius Caesar* and *Macbeth*, though, is that the action of assassination in Rome is supposedly more justifiable than in Scotland. Perhaps it's because Macbeth doesn't justify his cause with the powerful rhetoric of Brutus. It makes complete sense for terrorists to utilise rhetoric since deliberative rhetoric persuades listeners to approve of their opinion and disapprove of the victim's in order to take action, while forensic rhetoric persuades listeners to approve or condemn the past action itself. Both are vital for propaganda and become even more powerful if the speaker shows off their rhetorical prowess through epideictic rhetoric. The failing of Macbeth, so to speak, is that he does not understand the importance of spectacle and symbol in either speech or action. He is evil but he is not much of a terrorist, at least not a successful one.[11] If Macbeth was carrying out 9/11, he would not want cameras to capture it and he would not release a video claiming the attack. He perceives assassination to be a practical endeavour, not as Brutus or Booth understand it. When he asks "If we should fail?" (1.7.64), he also appears to be scared of being caught, not of failing to carry out the spectacular killing. He does not even regard King Duncan as a tyrant — quite the opposite: he sees his target as a man of "virtues" (1.7.18). Macbeth's action is therefore unsuccessful from the outset as it is centred in wholly individualistic motives, not relating to such issues as freedom or group identity — and uninterested in the spectacle. There is resultantly no Macbeth cult.

While language and action work hand in hand, when it comes to violence, the action does supersede the language. And even if the action is not fully realised, its symbolism carries it. *Julius Caesar* is thought to be the first play performed at the Globe, where the public model of theatre took flight and anybody could pay a penny to stand in the pit. This has led to an assumption, not entirely accurate but still valid, that some members of the audience "came along only for the spectacle, the language beyond their comprehension".[12] Shakespeare's Hamlet probably doesn't expect to be judged by his language but by his actions, unlike Brutus whose magnificent language in the play could well have overshadowed his actions. But the reality is that we usually think of Hamlet, who kills five (Polonius, Laertes, Claudius, Rosencrantz, and Guildenstern) and leads to the deaths of two more (Ophelia and Gertrude), as the contemplative monologist. But the rhetorician Brutus, who only killed one man hesitantly in a group attack, is entrenched as the assassin of Caesar – "Et tu, Brute?" (3.1.84). Perhaps that is the reason that ideologically, Hamlet has inspired justifications of terror. But practically, and especially when it comes to assassination, it is Brutus who has proved inspiring.

Five decades after Booth, *Julius Caesar* would also influence the attempted assassination of Hitler on 20 July 1944. Led by three figures in the German Army, the aim was to kill Hitler, arrest the leadership, and disarm the Schutzstaffel (SS). The assassination attempt itself was carried out by Claus von Stauffenberg, Chief of Staff for the Reserve Army, who planted a briefcase bomb at Hitler's headquarters in East Prussia. As a teenager some two decades earlier, and much like Booth, Stauffenberg had performed *Julius Caesar* with his two brothers. While his twin Alexander played Brutus and he played the servant Lucius, he became familiar with Brutus' motivations and justifications. Though the attempted operation was unsuccessful, it still had symbolic value. When Stauffenberg was arrested, he had an open copy of *Julius Caesar* on his desk, Brutus' lines underlined.[13]

That influence is not limited to Booth and Stauffenberg. Why is it, for instance, that Hitler sketched the scene of Julius Caesar's murder in his notepad? As mentioned in the first chapter, Gamal Abdel Nasser led the 1952 revolt against the Egyptian monarchy with his senior, General Muhammad Naguib. That coup removed the long-standing monarchy but wasn't the only one Nasser carried out. In the immediate aftermath, Naguib became prime minister with Nasser serving as interior minister. When Egypt became a republic in 1953, it was Naguib who became president. But he would last less than a year and a half as Nasser, previously his ally, removed him from power to become one of the most influential leaders of the twentieth century. Naguib remained under house arrest for almost two decades. Fascinatingly, Nasser knew *Julius Caesar* well; so well, in fact, that he played the title role as a sixteen-year-old in a well-attended school performance. As the emperor was about to be assassinated, biographers claim that Nasser's dad "seeing his eldest son fall beneath the dagger of Brutus, almost sprang up to the rescue".[14] Having attended less theatre than the middle classes, his father, a postman, may also have blurred the lines between drama and reality. What's more, according to the programme, the play presented Caesar as "a popular hero", a "conqueror of Great Britain ... assassinated as if by accident".[15] This reading of the play is curious but like the reaction of Nasser's father, indicates how the notion of overthrowing the leader, let alone killing him, was a shocking thought. Ironically, the minister of education was also in the audience; some years later he would become prime minister and Nasser would overthrow him. And Nasser would famously take on the Brutus role, so to speak, with the monarchy as well as his superior and ally Naguib – and indeed through his gripping rhetorical style.

It does make sense, then, for the assassination scene to cause unease. This is especially the case because the play has so often been adapted to contemporary contexts, exemplified by performances in the US in which a Caesar that looks like the president is assassinated, as Obama in 2012 and Donald Trump in 2017.[16] The Ethiopian emperor Haile Selassie "couldn't bear to watch the assassination scene" and in its 1952 Addis Ababa performance, "the Emperor's censors insisted that the scene be acted out behind a semidiaphanous curtain".[17] This even shares some similarities with early responses to the deposition scene in *Richard II*, where the king cedes his crown, which was censored from early editions of the play. By 1601, when conspirators including the Earl of Essex planned a deposition of Queen Elizabeth I, *Richard II* had become less popular in performance. The Earl paid 40 shillings to Shakespeare's company, a higher than usual fee, to put on a special performance of the play. They did so on the eve of the rebellion as a way of inspiring the conspirators, not least through the deposition scene. The plot failed and the conspirators were executed. Shakespeare's company got away with a warning.

THE GUNPOWDER BARD

If push factors (like retribution and grievance) and pull factors (like belonging and a greater cause) lead individuals to turn their ideology or language into action, just how did

Shakespeare understand this? In other words, how did this playwright from a small town feel equipped to construct and enter the minds of characters so careless of consequence and so imbued with a mission that they were ready to sacrifice everything? I would argue that this links directly to Shakespeare's own personal contexts and experiences.

First, Shakespeare was aware of the ubiquitous spy network in Elizabethan England. Sir Francis Walsingham, the zealous Protestant employed as the Queen's spymaster, created and ran an elaborate intelligence operation. This was essential in foiling plans like the Essex Rebellion, as well as plots from Catholic France and Spain. When Shakespeare was a child, Mary, Queen of Scots, was confined to Coventry, just twenty miles north of Stratford-upon-Avon. There were even plans to free Mary which were local but internationally planned alongside the Spanish ambassador, the Pope, Mary's ambassador in London, and Catholic lords. While this 1572 plot to free Mary and kill Elizabeth failed, Walsingham had released a key plotter, Roberto Ridolfi, so became adamant not to take any chances like that again. The tight surveillance network that existed around the English Midlands became even tighter. One can only wonder whether Shakespeare felt these confines first-hand. Aside from having artistic career ambitions beyond his town, could these contexts have made his England, including his Stratford, analogous with Hamlet's Elsinore? Like Hamlet, Shakespeare's personal escape was arguably through the power of acting. What's more, Catholics became mythologised as terrorists. Spain became mythologised as a terrorist state. Both of these were essentially done in the name of nationalism.

Importantly, and as I often find myself reminding students, Shakespeare was writing during both the Elizabethan and

Jacobean periods. As time went on, while succession became less of an issue, Spanish and Catholic influence and treason remained a threat. With issues of nationalism still at the fore since King James was the son of Mary, *Macbeth* engages with issues of English and Scottish nationalism. With its Scottish protagonist presented as a barbaric and violent traitor, it is only with the help of the English allies and the shedding of noble English blood (Young Siward's) that Macbeth can be defeated. And it is no secret that the subject of the play was picked specifically to please King James, who was also interested in witchcraft and ancestry.[18]

The perceived Catholic threat was something of which Shakespeare was very aware, in large part due to community and family ties. Violence was ever present, cries for the murder of kings and queens were in the air. The Throckmorton Plot to kill Elizabeth in 1583 was partly based around Coughton Court in Warwickshire. Indeed, both Elizabeth and James lived under constant threat and the papal bulls calling for their assassination meant Catholic sympathisers aroused suspicion. There has been endless discussion about Shakespeare's own beliefs. While he is likely to have stuck with the establishment view, he did have a Catholic background, not least his mother's Arden family. His father's activity as an official of the town corporation, when he was responsible for obliterating Catholic murals in the Guild Chapel, is also telling. This kind of iconoclasm is a tactic of terror, often from the state in order to suppress previous narratives, and it has occurred time and again over history (in the last decade, most notably by ISIS). Getting someone to destroy something they value themselves can be a further oppressive tactic (something East Jerusalemites have reported recently). Council records show that in 1563, John Shakespeare authorised payment of two shillings for "defasyng ymages in ye chappell". If John was simply carrying out his job, it indicates the importance of livelihood to the Shakespeare family (and his son may have embedded himself as part of the establishment in order to live a better life financially). If John tried to destroy the murals entirely, it poses questions about citizens' fear of being accused of loyalty to the old religion. John is thought to have scratched the murals at first before deciding to plaster over them. This lime-washing actually protected the paintings, so if this was his aim, it poses further questions about his potentially Catholic beliefs and loyalties.

At school, some of Shakespeare's teachers are likely to have been forced to step down due to Catholic sympathies. At this time, recusancy laws targeted recusants who refused to attend Church of England services and were therefore perceived as Catholic sympathisers. Notably, the English Midlands was the hub in which conspirators planned to blow up and overthrow the government. These included the homes of Robert Catesby and John Grant, both convicted in the Gunpowder Plot. Shakespeare's father, John, was friends with William Catesby, the father of Robert, the key conspirator. John and William even shared illegal Catholic writings that ended up in John's home. Through family and business ties, Shakespeare himself knew Grant, who had actually been involved in the Essex Rebellion a few years earlier. Other key conspirators included Thomas Percy, Christopher Wright, Guy Fawkes, and the Winter brothers, Robert and Thomas (who were also related to both Catesby and Grant). Mairi McDoland, a former archivist at Shakespeare's birthplace, studied the links in detail and found that fourteen of the nineteen men executed were related by marriage and all but one lived within thirty miles of Warwick over the previous twelve months. One of the plotters, Ambrose Rookwood, was at Clopton House just half a mile away from Shakespeare's home, where Shakespeare had also leased a property next door. The proximity of these events is made even clearer through a document of goods seized from Shakespeare's neighbour at Clopton House, which included religious (or Catholic) items like crucifixes and rosaries (Figure 4.2).[19]

Shakespeare is likely to have frequented the same taverns as the conspirators, too. He had maintained a link to his hometown, with his wife and children still residing there. He all but regarded it as home, living in modest accommodations in London while becoming one of the most prominent landowners in Stratford, also purchasing properties that included the second largest house in town, New Place (which he not only purchased but also renovated). That Stratford was at the centre of the Gunpowder Plot also meant that it became

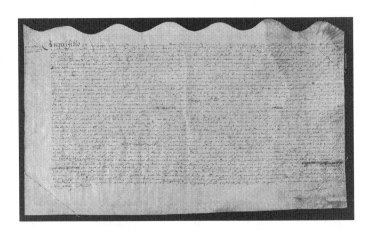

Figure 4.2 Inventory produced in an inquisition taken at Stratford-upon-Avon of the goods and chattels of Ambrose Rookwood, late attainted of High Treason, seized from Clopton House on 6 November 1605, 1606 (© Shakespeare Birthplace Trust).

something of a perceived terrorist hotspot in that it had increased surveillance. It was known as a "peculiar jurisdiction". Not participating in Holy Communion, for instance, aroused suspicion. Shakespeare's daughter, Susanna, is listed in a legal document from 1606 for failing to attend Easter mass. It is likely that she attended court and apologised formally.

Many of these links between Shakespeare and the conspirators are well known.[20] But the link between Shakespeare's son-in-law and the conspirators has been comparatively mute. John Hall was a Stratford-based Puritan physician who married Susanna Shakespeare. In 2020, Hall's complete medical notes were combined and published for the first time. Here, we get a sense of Hall's interaction with two conspirators, Robert and Thomas Winter. Hall's entry for case 103 notes a cure for scurvy for "Mrs Mary Talbot, a gentlewoman, sister of the Earl, Roman Catholic, modest and well-conducted". She was daughter of Sir John Talbot, from a wealthy Catholic family linked through marriage to several local recusant families. And her older sister Gertrude was married to Robert Winter.[21] The entry suggests Hall's common personal and professional interactions with recusants. These were often very direct. Case 119, from 1623 or 1624, confirms interaction with Margaret Winter, who had a flux from the belly and whom he describes as "Mrs Winter, gentlewoman, a widow aged 28, Roman Catholic".[22] She was the wife of John Winter, Robert Winter's son. The family's estate was not immediately forfeited to the crown when the Winters were convicted in the Gunpowder Plot, but did get taken from Gertrude for recusancy in 1607. The family regained the estate around 1622. This interaction, then, shows that Shakespeare's son-in-law kept good relations with the Winter family even after the Gunpowder Plot and recusancy charges. As far as Shakespeare is concerned, he had a close relationship with his son-in-law, "they travelled to London together" and "Hall probably treated Shakespeare" in his last days. Shakespeare named him and Susanna as residuary beneficiaries of his estate and they "inherited the bulk", including New Place.[23] This relationship further confirms Shakespeare's tangible proximity to the local community members and acquaintances responsible for the Gunpowder Plot.

The introduction to this book alluded to the fact that the Gunpowder Plot is a helpful way of reading Shakespeare as a post-terror respondent to the events of his time. Readings of *Macbeth* as an establishment response condemning the Gunpowder Plot are valid, as are those which articulate the play's complicated responses to contemporary events.[24] Particularly important is Peter C. Herman's thesis that *Macbeth*, perhaps revised before its Folio publication, presents a view of terrorism as "A deed without a name" (4.1.49). This emphasis on the "unspeakable" nature of terrorism allows it to have unprecedented and devastating aims and impacts.[25]

It can hardly be overstated that the events of the early 1600s signified an unusual and pivotal time in the country's history. As the plotting activity intensified, Nicolò Molino, the Venetian ambassador, reported that the "king is in terror".[26] The scale of what the plot aimed to achieve is monumental: a seventeenth-century equivalent of 9/11 involving thirty-six barrels of gunpowder that would have devastated London. The king told Molino:

> Had the scheme been carried out thirty-thousand persons would have perished at a stroke, the city would have been sacked ... in short, the world have seen a spectacle so terrible and terrifying that it's like has never been heard of.[27]

It was no doubt impossible for Shakespeare to ignore such an event in his writing even if he chose to distance himself from it ideologically. But it is also possible to link *Macbeth* to some of the key issues related to our perceptions and receptions of terrorism today. First, in how tropes and terminology related to terrorism were and continue to be embedded into popular cultural responses (like *Macbeth* then and Hollywood movies today). Second, in some of the parallels that the real and fictional events share with current narratives around terrorism.

Indeed, the government, led by the king, reacted by making their official stance and narrative clear through religious and political propaganda. The king commemorated the foiling of the plot by commissioning a silver medal that pictures a snake hiding amidst flowers. It makes sense, then, for Lady Macbeth to tell her husband to "look like th'innocent flower, / But be the serpent under't" (1.5.66–67). In the weeks that followed, the words "train" and "blow" became related to the Plot and could not be used innocently any more, much like the word "bomb" today, so their usage in *Macbeth* would have caught the audience's attention. Garry Wills elucidates many such examples in the play from start to end.[28] Even the official handbill (Figure 4.3) communicated "By the King" is telling. Published on 7 November – just hours after Guy Fawkes was caught and as an army was being sent to Warwickshire – the start of this "wanted list" containing the conspirators' names reads:

> Whereas Thomas Percy Gentleman, and some other his confederates, persons knowen to be bitterly corrupted with the superstition of the Romish Religion, as seduced with the blindness thereof, and being otherwise of lewde life, insolent disposition, and for the most part of desperate estate,

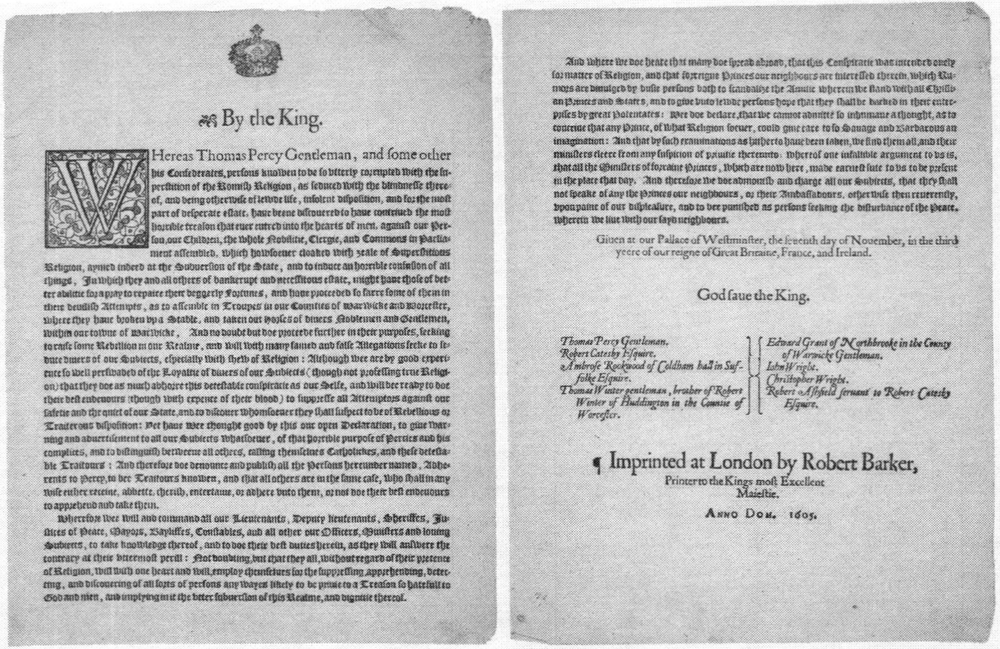

By the King.

WHereas Thomas Percy Gentleman, and some other his Confederates, persons knowen to be so vtterly corrupted with the superstition of the Romish Religion, as seduced with the blindnesse thereof, and being otherwise of lewde life, insolent disposition, and for the most part of desperate estate, haue beene discouered to haue contriued the most horrible treason that euer entred into the hearts of men, against our Person, our Children, the whole Nobilitie, Clergie, and Commons in Parliament assembled, which howsoeuer cloaked with zeale of Superstitious Religion, aymed indeed at the Subuersion of the State, and to induce an horrible confusion of all things, In which they and all others of bankerupt and necessitous estate, might haue those of better abilitie for a pray to repaire their beggerly Fortunes, and haue proceeded so farre some of them in their deuilish Attempts, as to assemble in Troupes in our Counties of Warwicke and Worcester, where they haue broken vp a Stable, and taken out horses of diuers Noblemen and Gentlemen, within our towne of Warwicke, And no doubt but doe proceede further in their purposes, seeking to raise some Rebellion in our Realme, and will with many fained and false Allegations seeke to seduce diuers of our Subiects, especially with shew of Religion: Although wee are by good experience so well perswaded of the Loyaltie of diuers of our Subiects (though not professing true Religion) that they doe as much abhorre this detestable conspiracie as our Selfe, and will bee ready to doe their best endeuours (though with expence of their blood) to suppresse all Attemptors against our safetie and the quiet of our State, and to discouer whomsoeuer they shall suspect to be of Rebellious or Traiterous disposition: Yet haue wee thought good by this our open Declaration, to giue warning and aduertisement to all our Subiects whatsoeuer, of that horrible purpose of Percie and his complices, and to distinguish betweene all others, calling themselues Catholickes, and these detestable Traitours: And therefore doe denounce and publish all the Persons hereunder named, Adherents to Percy, to bee Traitours knowen, and that all others are in the same case, who shall in any wise either receiue, abbette, cherish, entertaine, or adhere vnto them, or not doe their best endeuours to apprehend and take them.

Wherefore Wee will and command all our Lieutenants, Deputy lieutenants, Sheriffes, Justices of Peace, Mayors, Bayliffes, Constables, and all other our Officers, Ministers and louing Subiects, to take knowledge thereof, and to doe their best duties herein, as they will answere the contrary at their vttermost perill: Not doubting, but that they all, without regard of their pretence of Religion, will with one heart and will, employ themselues for the suppressing, apprehending, detecting, and discouering of all sorts of persons any wayes likely to be priuie to a Treason so hatefull to God and men, and implying in it the vtter subuersion of this Realme, and dignitie thereof.

And where we doe heare that many doe spread abroad, that this Conspiracie was intended onely for matter of Religion, and that forreigne Princes our neighbours are interessed therein, which Rumors are diuulged by busie persons both to scandalize the Amitie wherein we stand withall Christian Princes and States, and to giue vnto lewde persons hope that they shall be backed in their enterprises by great Potentates: Wee doe declare, that we cannot admitte so inhumane a thought, as to conceiue that any Prince, of what Religion soeuer, could giue eare to so Sauage and Barbarous an imagination: And that by such examinations as hitherto haue been taken, we find them all, and their ministers cleere from any suspicion of priuitie thereunto: whereof one infallible argument to vs is, that all the Ministers of forraine Princes, which are now here, made earnest suite to vs to be present in the place that day. And therefore we doe admonish and charge all our Subiects, that they shall not speake of any the Princes our neighbours, or their Ambassadours, otherwise then reuerently, vpon paine of our displeasure, and to bee punished as persons seeking the disturbance of the Peace, wherein we liue with our sayd neighbours.

Giuen at our Pallace of Westminster, the seuenth day of Nouember, in the third yeere of our reigne of Great Britaine, France, and Ireland.

God saue the King.

Thomas Percy Gentleman.
Robert Catesby Esquire.
Ambrose Rockwood of Coldham hall in Suffolke Esquire.
Thomas Winter gentleman, brother of Robert Winter of Huddington in the Countie of Worcester.
Edward Grant of Northbrooke in the County of Warwicke Gentleman.
Iohn Wright.
Christopher Wright.
Robert Ashfield seruant to Robert Catesby Esquire.

¶ Imprinted at London by Robert Barker, Printer to the Kings most Excellent Maiestie.

ANNO DOM. 1605.

Figure 4.3 Printed proclamation for the apprehension of the chief conspirators in the Gunpowder Plot, 1605 (© Shakespeare Birthplace Trust).

have beene discovered to have contrived the most horrible
treason that ever entered into the hearts of men, against
our Person, our Children, the whole Nobilitie, Clergie, and
Commons in Parliament assembled, which howsoever
cloaked with zeale of Superstitious Religion, aymed indeed
at the Subversion of the State, and to induce an horrible
confusion of all things.[29]

This handbill would have appeared all over the country and
especially Stratford, been read aloud in markets, pinned to
doors and trees. The language here is unequivocal. It denotes
terrorism: its ambition, collectiveness, subversion, symbolism, and religious motivation. Further parallels with
today include the notion that those Catholics who love the
king have nothing to worry about; it is only the extremists
who are being targeted. But law-abiding Catholics would still
have been apprehensive about the potential suppression to
follow after an event they had nothing to do with but that
was carried out in their name. Moreover, there is a call on
the public to be vigilant and provide information about anything suspicious (also repeated on loudspeakers at Stratford's
railway station today). In places of worship and education,
the UK government's controversial Prevent scheme obliges
preachers and teachers to report information to government.
The priest Henry Garnet, who was executed for his part in the
plot, claimed that he was bound by the seal of confession (the
absolute duty not to disclose information heard at penance).

But perhaps it was another terror plot, again an assassination attempt, that confirmed Shakespeare's intention to
engage so directly with these contemporary events. In 1606,
reports of the king's alleged assassination spread across the
country, only for the rumours to be quashed and for him

to be celebrated as though he had been resurrected.[30] It is fitting that the word "assassination" takes flight in *Macbeth*. According to the *Oxford English Dictionary*, Shakespeare appears to have coined it from the noun "assassin".[31] This moment gave Shakespeare the potential for a two-pronged approach in *Macbeth* so that he could show his indignation at both the Gunpowder Plot and the assassination of the king, both his loyalty to the nation and the leaders, both Parliament and monarchy. "Murder *and* treason!" (2.3.72; emphasis mine), as Macduff puts it in his shock, allowed Shakespeare to both condemn the Gunpowder Plot, and through the hagiographic representation of King Duncan, present his reverence for the king and the establishment.

Treason and assassination were so serious that the English Treason Act of 1351 specifies: "When a Man doth compass or *imagine* the Death of our Lord the King" (emphasis mine). Today, we see similar ideas with terrorism: airports that have posters about the prison sentence for "joking about terrorism" and terror-related crimes include "planning, assisting and even collecting information" about an attack, not only carrying one out. Aside from this parallel, what was Shakespeare doing putting so much treason and assassination on the stage? With metatheatre at the centre of his art and drama, showing the death of a monarch on stage is surely a way of imagining it. When taking this context into consideration, it does make sense for Shakespeare to be taking sides in order to maintain this liberty to entertain using, essentially, whatever topic he pleases. It is therefore convincing that the death of Macbeth is a directly didactic moment in his works, something that does not happen too often in the oeuvre.[32] By the end, the character's severed head serves as a symbolic spectacle. But even from the start, when Macbeth finds that the witches may be right and that he might therefore become king, even before he has plotted against Duncan he sighs that "Present fears / Are less than horrible imaginings" (1.3.147–48). Macbeth knows that he is committing treason by simply visualising the prospect of taking the throne. When we see Macbeth struggling with justification for his ruthless ambition, then, we are listening to key words and tropes inspired by reports of the Gunpowder Plot. And in our potential sympathy for the protagonist, we may just be identifying with a terrorist.

After Elizabeth's death in 1603, Shakespeare was asked to write a new scene for the play *Sir Thomas More*, a play so controversial it hadn't yet been performed and is unlikely to have seen the stage during his lifetime. In the scene – the only surviving play script in Shakespeare's handwriting – anti-immigration rioters in London protest the number of French Protestants seeking asylum in the capital. Through Shakespeare's quill, More – Henry VIII's chancellor – calls on the crowds to show sympathy towards the refugees, or as they're called in the text, the "strangers". He asks the protesters what they'd do if they were one day evicted from England. "Whither would you go? / What country, by the nature of your error, / Should give you harbour?" (6.141–43). He continues, "Would you be pleased to find a nation of such barbarous temper, / That ... would not afford you an abode on earth?" (6.147–49), explaining to them that *they* would then be the immigrants and refugees. More's actual opinion might have been more subtle:

> It is not our intents to drive away or expel any distressed strangers out of our land, but to have them live here, that we might be able to live with them and that they should live under government and to be obedient to good orders.[33]

This could mean that those who were no longer seeking asylum were not welcome. It also confirms that absolutes don't really exist: although there was some sympathy towards Protestants struggling in Europe, they were expected to live on English terms and integrate. This unrest about immigration reemerged during Elizabeth's reign and while the play's fascinating speech cannot confirm Shakespeare's personal opinions, it nonetheless shows both humanity and diplomacy. It is a telling example of how Shakespeare wanted to put politics on the stage but refused to deal in absolute opinions.

These kinds of contexts, not least the extreme violence and religious divisions Shakespeare witnessed throughout his life, had an irrevocable effect on his writing.[34] On one hand, murder, and specifically, murder of the ruler, was a real threat. Shakespeare was bound to engage with it in order to make his plays topical – and because it makes good drama. A great number of plots are concerned with the accession or disposition of a monarch or duke. On another, Shakespeare had become part of the establishment and was on the side of the crown and was engaged with the monarchy in a professional capacity. He therefore wanted to distance himself from the actions of his acquaintances and the plots that developed in his home county. Fernie summarises his view of the playwright's response to the Gunpowder Plot insightfully and tactfully: "I don't see Shakespeare as absolutely partisan in that case ... nor do I see him as totally objective and paring his fingernails beyond the heat of faction and contemption".[35]

Perhaps these contexts can enable us to see a more holistic Shakespeare. Far from romanticising him as some sort of neutral ideal, this actually creates further ambiguity in his works. Shakespeare was both a citizen and a celebrity, a Stratfordian and a Londoner, someone who understood his townspeople's perspectives but also wanted to impress the royals and become part of the establishment, a man who knew his Catholic background but felt his status transcended the need to even engage with it – one imagines something of an O. J. Simpson conception: "I'm not Catholic, I'm Shakespeare".

EPILOGUE: THE IMPERMANENCE OF TRUTH

Like the 9/11 bombers, like Booth, the Gunpowder plotters believed they had a duty to rise up against and free themselves from an illegitimate or oppressive force. They had a moral duty: a cause, a grievance, and a spiritual inclination. To them, their beliefs and opinions represented an ultimate truth. But looking at these in and around Shakespeare indicates that truth is impermanent: an important inference in today's post-truth world.

The truth is often a lie. It can be, and always has been, a tool for those in attempting to gain or cement power. But like power, truth is impermanent. Even what appears to be absolute can turn out to be relative. Some previously empirical truths are now conceptual or even metaphysical. My generation would have been penalised for excluding Pluto from the list of planets. True then, false now. Galileo Galilei, the famous Italian astronomer, challenged seventeenth-century Europe's beliefs that the earth was the centre of the universe and that it doesn't move, insisting that the sun is at the centre and that the earth moves around it. The Church wasn't impressed, and in 1633, he was forced to retract his theories and convicted of heresy, spending the rest of his life under house arrest. Granted, these are realities of scientific enquiry, but they remain fine examples of the temporality of what we name a fact. In a way, fact manipulation and "fake news" are nothing new. And they can be used to instigate ideological warfare, whether in the name of terror or counter-terror. Shakespeare presents clear "post-truth" politics in *Julius Caesar*, for instance, when the ruler's murderers are able to justify their treachery to the public using focused rhetoric. But perhaps false or manipulated facts have now become epidemic in extent and reach, with quick-fire tweeting by commoners and influencers – plebeians and patricians with blue ticks for blue blood – alike such a norm that our relationship with truth is becoming vaguer by the day.

So, how did this playwright from a small town feel equipped to construct and enter the minds of characters so careless of consequence? He knew that humans seek freedom, that they believe their ideas to be ultimate truths, and that sometimes they act on these notions. As Fernie puts it, he understood what it meant to have "extreme feeling and the imperatives to do extraordinary things".[36]

That imperative is almost always some sort of freedom, like Cinna's proclamation: "Liberty! Freedom! Tyranny is dead!" (3.1.85). Fascinatingly, when the New York performance with Caesar as Trump was interrupted immediately after these lines, the woman who took to the stage shouted: "You guys are ISIS!". Linking a Shakespearean performance to a terrorist organisation speaks to the way in which the play and its myriad adaptations, as well as the audience's own preconceptions and interpretations, can certainly affect sensibilities and emotions. Similarly, that and subsequent performances were linked with Nazi propaganda: "You are all Joseph Goebbels. You are inciting terrorists". But most revealingly, the audience member who interrupted the play also said, "Stop the normalization of political violence against the right".[37] Shakespeare's interaction with political violence is undeniable. Both the historical events and dramatic plots confirm that by nature, Shakespeare is politicised – in his time and in turn, at any time. But his comprehension of the potential for extreme feeling informs how he confronts issues of political violence both in his life and on the stage: he explores them but stops short of support or condemnation. It makes sense, then, for him to be utilised by any side of the spectrum and for some terrorists to love him as much as some despise him. Shakespeare shows awareness of the human potential for polarisation through the relationships of protagonists with antagonists, through the differences between characters' public and private roles, through civil wars, and more. That potential for civil tension and personal extremity is shown in perhaps the most striking stage direction in the oeuvre, in Act Two of *Henry VI, Part 3*: "*Alarum. Enter a son that has killed his father, at one door, and a father that hath killed his son at another door [with their bodies]*" (2.5). And Shakespeare's understanding of the consequences of tension and violence are exemplified in *King John* as Lady Constance personifies grief's existence as the presence of both the deceased after they are gone and the bereaved as they live on (3.4.95–107).

But as the events show, both then and now, when it comes to a struggle for freedom and truth, we often find an enactment ensuing on and between contradictory terms. The tragic hero, for one, is neither fully good nor fully bad and the audience usually sympathises and scorns that protagonist in equal measure. In *Hamlet*, Polonius tells Reynaldo that lying is the best way of reaching the truth:

Your bait of falsehood takes this carp of truth:
And thus do we of wisdom and of reach,

> With windlasses and with assays of bias,
> By indirections find directions out:
>
> (2.1.65–68)

Such a contradiction might just be what Shakespeare learns and presents from the events of his time. As Herman argues with *Macbeth*, Shakespeare neither sympathises with the terrorists nor, as many would have it, goes all out with state propaganda. While maintaining some value system, he nonetheless presents both sides of that story, both its public and private issues. The play therefore begins with the witches' "Fair is foul, and foul is fair" (1.1.12) and Macbeth's famous first words: "So foul and fair a day I have not seen" (1.39). Among other links, Lancelot Andrewes' sermons, commissioned by the king in the aftermath of the Gunpowder Plot, used these terms. The plan itself was foul in its intent and fair in its discovery. Shakespeare alludes to the complexity of these events: like the serpent under the flower, they may not always be as simple as they appear. Like Milton's Satan disguising as a serpent to Eve, evil can appear attractive, so one cannot jump to immediate conclusions about those who fall into the trappings of evil actions, but rather, try to understand why they reached that state. Milton, in fact, was fascinated by the Gunpowder Plot growing up and wrote poems about it, as well as presenting gunpowder as a demonic tool used by Satan in *Paradise Lost*. In both the temptation of Eve and the potential attractiveness of Satan, Milton presents an entirely complicated perception of truth in his epic poem.

The complications in both Shakespeare and Milton are not so much in the paradox of good versus evil (or fair versus foul), but rather, how one might be required in order for the other to exist. In *Paradise Lost*, as in the Abrahamic traditions, the theodical paradigm is such that the existence of evil (in the form of Satan) justifies the actions, importance, and superiority of good (in the form of God). A similar paradigm extends to freedom, which only comes into the world really when evil is introduced (whether in the form of the tempter who provides Adam and Eve with a new option, or the evil of the forbidden fruit itself). In theory, restrained from evil, humans risk a lack of ambition and a blunted sense of identity. They risk being un-free.

NOTES

1 I am grateful to Paul Edmondson, Erin Sullivan, Katie Brokaw, Matt Stead, and Karen Harker for their insights on this event.
2 Katie Brokaw, in conversation with Islam Issa (January 2021).
3 Helen Hopkins, "'Gifts of the World'?".
4 Ibid.
5 Nora Titone, *My Thoughts Be Bloody* (New York: Free Press, 2010), 338.
6 Ibid., 340.
7 Ibid., 14.
8 Fernie, in Issa, "Shakespeare and Terrorism", BBC Radio 3.
9 I use the term "basic" because Lincoln was not an absolute abolitionist whose views developed; see Eric Foner, *The Fiery Trial: Abraham Lincoln and American Slavery* (New York: W. W. Norton, 2010). Also, historian Jill Lepore, in *These Truths: A History of the United States* (New York: W. W. Norton, 2018), argues that many people harboured a co-existence of pro-slavery but pro-US-freedom sentiment.
10 Albert Furtwangler, *Assassin on Stage: Brutus, Hamlet, and the Death of Lincoln* (Urbana: University of Illinois Press, 1991), 98.
11 G. Wilson Knight, *The Wheel of Fire*, calls Macbeth "Shakespeare's most profound and mature vision of evil", 140. Graham Holderness, *Tales from Shakespeare*, 198–205, presents Macbeth as a terrorist due to his irrational commitment to the deed, but this reading does not consider the multiple factors at play in the terrorist mindset.
12 Sean McEvoy, *Shakespeare: The Basics* (London: Routledge, 2006), 14.

13 Andreas Höfele, *No Hamlets: German Shakespeare from Nietzsche to Carl Schmitt* (Oxford: Oxford University Press, 2016), 192.

14 Jean Lacouture, *Nasser: A Biography*, trans. Daniel Hofstadter (New York: Knopf, 1973), 29.

15 Ibid.

16 See Jeffrey R. Wilson, *Shakespeare and Trump* (Philadelphia: Temple University Press, 2020), 129–85.

17 Hussein Omar, "Hamlet's Arab Journey", Bidoun 26 (Fall 2011), www.bidoun.org/articles/margaret-litvin-hamlet-s-arab-journey-shakespeare-s-prince-and-nasser-s-ghost [accessed 29 January 2021].

18 Kenneth Muir, "Introduction", in *Macbeth*, by William Shakespeare (London: Methuen, 1980), liv.

19 "Copy of the inquisition of the Bailiff of Stratford-upon-Avon as to the goods seized at Clopton House, with inventory and valuation", 26 February 1606 (Shakespeare Birthplace Trust PR385/6); "Inventory produced in an inquisition taken at Stratford-upon-Avon of the goods and chattels of Ambrose Rookewoode [Rookwood], late attainted of High Treason, seized from Clopton House on 6 November 1605", 26 February 1606 (Shakespeare Birthplace Trust ER27/14).

20 On both the Catholic question and Shakespeare's links to conspirators, see Shapiro, 1606.

21 Greg Wells and Paul Edmondson, *John Hall Master of Physicke: A Casebook from Shakespeare's Stratford* (Manchester: Manchester University Press, 2020), 167.

22 Ibid., 188.

23 Stanley Wells, "Foreword", in Wells and Edmondson, *John Hall*, xvi.

24 On one hand, Barker, *The Culture of Violence*; Holderness and Loughrey, "Shakespeare and Terror". On another, Wills, *Witches & Jesuits*; Herman, *Unspeakable*; Lemon, *Treason by Words*; Shapiro, 1606; Harris, "The Smell of Gunpowder".

25 Herman, *Unspeakable*, 6, 19–34.

26 Shapiro, 1606, 115.

27 Ibid.

28 Wills, *Witches & Jesuits*, 19–31. The link to today's term, "bomb", was clear in the Globe's *Shakespeare and the Gunpowder Plot* exhibition (2005), curated by Nick de Somogyi, which included a mocked-up

contemporary Metropolitan Police incident board appealing for information from the public about a "Bomb Scare" on "5th Nov 1605".

29 "Printed proclamation for the apprehension of the chief conspirators in the Gunpowder Plot", 7 November 1605 (Shakespeare Birthplace Trust ER123).

30 Shapiro, 1606, 233–38.

31 David Roberts, "Shakespeare and Terrorism", in *Terrorism and the Arts: Practices and Critiques in Contemporary Cultural Production*, ed. Jonathan Harris (London: Routledge, 2021).

32 See Lemon, *Treason by Words*, 84.

33 John Jowett, "Introduction", *Sir Thomas More* (London: Bloosmbury, 2017), 43. Quotations from the play are from this edition.

34 For a detailed study of such instances, see Lake, *How Shakespeare Put Politics on the Stage*.

35 Fernie, in Issa, "Shakespeare and Terrorism", BBC Radio 3.

36 Ibid.

37 Wilson, *Shakespeare and Trump*, 175–77.

THE HUMAN STRUGGLE

In the twentieth century alone, humans killed more than 100 million fellow humans, not to mention the physical and emotional torture and injustice humans have forced on one another and the violence inflicted on other sentient beings and on nature. If Shakespeare did indeed explore or understand what it means to be a human, then an integral part of that is a portrayal of the pain, trauma, and terror that we are capable of creating as individuals and as a collective species.

Every day, as we chat to friends and family, as we scan the news and social media feed, as we observe the natural world during a nice stroll, as we order our favourite coffees, and as we actively or passively receive art in its multiple forms, we are essentially making hundreds of rapid moral judgements. Do I like this or not? Do I agree or disagree? At the most fundamental levels, we are adding pieces to our individual jigsaws and determining who we actually are. We are undertaking the most vital human activity: interpretation.

The magnitude of these moral judgements might be even more accentuated in a world that continues to perpetuate inequalities based on gender, race, ability, class, sexuality, faith, nationality, and more. Just what do we have to say and do in order to survive and better yet to emerge on the right side of the tumultuous moral tests of our time? In an increasingly

DOI: 10.4324/9780429320088-6

polarised world where endless opinions and histories are more accessible than ever and wafer-thin margins decide political landscapes, can we identify with the appropriate worldviews and disidentify from the troublesome ones so as to boast a seemingly "spotless reputation" (a phrase coined in *Richard II*)? And at a time in which mighty echo chambers encompass us in both the physical and digital locales (sometimes intertwined, such as Google search suggestions based on location), can we maintain a grip on what is true and differentiate it from what is cataclysmically false? Anything open to interpretation is also open to misinterpretation.

The struggle for interpretation might be the key crossover between life and art.

It is made especially difficult due to the multitude of influences around us. These include the mighty weight of socialisation and first impressions as well as the contested and impermanent nature of truth.

When it comes to truth, the discussion in this book has been intended as a spark. First, a challenge to assumptions about that dominant narrative or single interpretation of pretty much anything, not least cultural and canonical icons. We cannot assume that a single Shakespearean figure or oeuvre exists — or a single way of reading, performing, watching, or utilising his work. The same issues of assumption apply to history, politics, and sociology — particularly of places, people, and phenomena that are so often orientalised as exotic and inferior, and that are very often reported from an outsider's lens and victim to assumptive prejudices and discrimination. Alternative narratives can shift and morph through space and time, in turn probing the concept of truth.

It takes us just one-tenth of a second to make a judgement about the person in front of us. Shakespeare constructs characters that show awareness of this and in turn complicate it. In *As You Like It*, Phoebe asks: "Who ever loved that loved not at first sight?" (3.5.81). But ironically, the man she's fallen in love with is the disguised Rosalind. So maybe it's Romeo who's onto something when he ponders how "Love is a smoke made with the fume of sighs" (1.1.179). Indeed, first impressions affect us daily. The two traits we detect quickest in human faces are attractiveness, and believe it or not, trust-worthiness. Unconscious biases are often responses to what we see at first sight, like gender or race. Studies in the US and Europe have proven that people are more likely to think a black male is about to shoplift, or that a woman with a tattoo on her back is more promiscuous. In *The Tempest*, the only humans Miranda has ever met on the remote island are her father and Caliban. When she sees Ferdinand, she emits the simplest of phrases: "What is't?" (1.2.474). These simple monosyllabic words show Miranda's naivety on one hand, but her desire and wonderment on the other. But Miranda's question, "What is it?", is more than just characterisation: essentially, it's the question of the entire Renaissance. What is life? What is art? What is morality? And if we read it most literally, what is a human? First impressions reconnect us to life's biggest questions. But they also risk developing into echo chambers of prejudice, into distortions of reality, as demonstrated, for instance, by repeatedly anti-Semitic Nazi performances of *The Merchant of Venice*. In that play, Shakespeare also shows understanding of the interpretative first impression. The Prince of Morocco attempting to court Portia might have high status back home, but even he knows that he must overcome presumption, entering with the words: "Mislike me not for my complexion" (2.1.1). Impressions often establish someone's value; even a prince can feel the need to justify his own presence.

But there is also something to be said about conformism. As those crowds in Shakespeare's addition to *Sir Thomas More* indicate, we are more likely to formulate our views in line with majority opinion. It's another reason we have ivory towers and echo chambers. With Shakespeare, this is intensified because there are multiple players involved, not just the playwright, actors, audience members, and reader. Directors can also control our interpretive first impressions. In a recent adaptation of *Macbeth* in Pakistan, lighting dictated this. A specific signature colour was assigned for each character: deep blue lighting for the witches to evoke a sense of desire, intensifying their power to seduce Macbeth. After his first encounter with them, Macbeth's signature pale white lighting turned blue to show their grip on him. Red lighting emphasised tragic moments: when Macbeth contemplated murdering the king, a red light was cast over him, repeated when Macbeth is killed at the end.

The variety of colours used to codify the characters made me wonder how quickly we make our first impressions and how they're not always objective, but often imposed by society. Maybe we should be asking: what colours do we assign to ourselves, and to those around us? We might only have milliseconds to decide.[1]

RESISTANT RECEPTION, ENTRY POINTS, AND PERIPHERY NEGLECT

The human struggle for interpretation is no bad thing, certainly not when it comes to literature. As my thinking on

195 **Epilogue**

reception has progressed, I have developed a differentiation between the work and the text. A work includes the text, as well as contexts, responses, and in Shakespeare's case, afterlives and legacies. In a way, we have to accept that the text does not change in and of itself. If the text rarely changes, what does? Readings of the text change. In turn, the meanings or essences of a text can be altered. The field of literary reception is not just a way of analysing literature, it is an appreciation and rejuvenation of artistic life and potential. It is part of the strife towards understanding the text. After all, "different responses … do not reciprocally falsify one another, but rather, testify to the historically progressive concretisation of meaning in the struggle for interpretation".[2]

RESISTANT RECEPTION

This emphasis on the work, not just the text, indicates the need to think about modes of reception that extend beyond reading per se. In particular, when it comes to groups who have long been marginalised, such as women and people of colour, resistant reading has served as a way of moving away from the normative expectations of a text, such as feeling antipathy rather than sympathy for the male or white character. Now, a move to what I term *resistant reception* is important in order to appreciate, first, the power of a work, not just a text, and second, the different intersections and players active in our everyday spaces and cultural contexts. As a result of education systems, colonialism, popular culture, and more, Shakespeare's presence, importance, and influence are a result of more than simply his texts. As such, *resistant reception* is more likely to take into account his impact on formal education, his inclusion in the colonial project, and his popular cultural legacy. This is possible because *resistant reception* expands and links the work to wider issues outside of the text itself; in Shakespeare's case, this might include questioning ideas of cultural hegemony and hierarchy as well his assumed popularity and canonicity. What is more, by rejuvenating the reception process beyond the confines of interpreting plot and character, we become more likely to respond actively to a work's relationship with the key and fast developing issues of our time, moving from observers of racism in the world of a text to anti-racist allies in the real world, from appreciating the existence of beauty ideals to redefining them, from being aware of sexual harassment to calling it out.

Taking account of reception rather than reading per se also brings vital nuance and varied voices into the conversation, from translators and directors worldwide to those who have not even read Shakespeare (remember, most book burners or terrorists don't read the literature they detest, but their impact on its afterlife is tangible).[3] In fact, since the specific action of reading sadly remains a privilege in many parts of the world and more so for women, *resistant reception* is a more collective and inclusive phenomenon that also allows further marginalised groups into the conversation. For instance, I recall meeting in 2007 an illiterate woman in rural Egypt (my friends and I tried her home for fish bait when we ran out and she insisted that we eat with her family). After finding out that I study English literature, she bellowed Shakespeare's name beamingly. Isn't she affected by Shakespeare's work since Britain occupied Egypt and in fact, a key battle of the 1882 Anglo-Egyptian War took place just miles from where she lives?

As introduced in the first chapter, then, *resistant reception* has the ability to develop beyond resistant reading's focus on the world of the fiction by linking the work both to its fictional world and the real world around it — something particularly important with Shakespeare.

ENTRY POINTS

That being said, I believe that when it comes to reception, literary critics in particular are required to take steps back in order to take steps forward. We are, fundamentally, entering the literary conversation from an inadequate or at least dubious entry point. Crudely put, to understand the myriad and holistic ways in which we seek meaning from literature, a different entry point to the usual scholarship is required, a different springboard. This is necessary in order to continuously ask important questions about Shakespeare. Are we passively accepting the normalised narratives? Are we basing the work and its afterlife on nonchalant historical myths about popularity, universality, and canonicity? Are we giving validity to lesser known viewpoints?

PERIPHERY NEGLECT

Some readers and audiences, however, are assumed to be on the peripheries or shunned towards them, therefore ignored at the expense of mainstream readers and audiences whose assumptions and readings carry more weight and precedence. I have termed this phenomenon *periphery neglect*. These mainstream responses (often from white, English-speaking males, mostly affiliated to traditional institutions and publishers) also influence and further hegemonise mainstream interpretations and narratives, not only related to culture and the arts, but also to history, including sociological and political events.

This book advances the theory of *periphery neglect* by confirming that the periphery reader is often the insignificant significant reader, one that is real rather than implied. Different recipients of Shakespeare, through their varying, intersectional identity categories and life experiences, can be the missing link that confirms the ways in which the literature spills into and out of the real world. Such reception can have real consequences.

To give a stark example, Ayatollah Khamenei is no literary critic and certainly not a mainstream one. But by acknowledging his perspective, the meanings created by the literature advance even further. To some Western governments, Iran may represent an axis of evil. In the meantime, Khamenei is using Shakespeare, a Western icon, to advance his own ideology in Iran. That is the very same ideology that Western governments claim they have been trying to decipher and continue attempting to undermine. And yet, by neglecting Khamenei since he is a periphery reader, one could argue that they are allowing him to advance his own ideology while not even getting close to figuring it out themselves. As such, *periphery neglect* has wider implications, in this case related to national security.[4]

THE INTENTIONAL VITALITY

What was Shakespeare trying to do? Much in the same way that writers are themselves readers (and we know this of Shakespeare), when composing his plays and poems, Shakespeare must have undergone his own interpretative activity. This would have included his own personal exploration of the world around him as well as a commercial analysis of what would please his audiences. As such, one thing that Shakespeare boasts is the ability to both explore human nature *and* to entertain.[5] But that also necessitates an awareness often taken for granted: that his plots and themes are not only explorative or attractive, but both.

Shakespeare did want his characters and especially his central ones to be appealing – even if (or maybe even because) they upset nature and sensibility through an ability to commit despicable or violent acts. That much is easy to say. It is more difficult to decode why that makes good theatre and what the appeal has been for audiences over the centuries. What's more, how do we account for what spills into the real world: when the (righteous) indignation and (acceptable) madness that happen on the stage don't stay within the confines of the theatre, but begin to affect the world outside it? Or when the actual text becomes so much less influential than the work and its afterlife?

Part of the answer to why the plays are at once explorative, attractive, and timeless is their vitality. Terrorists fit into a wider social framework and narrative. They turn their words into actions. Their actions affect many others. The actions are often responses – and these result in further responses. In a similar manner, the protagonist of a play is just one aspect, one story within the complex and hidden world of that play. The protagonist turns words into action. Their actions are often a response and they usually result in further responses. They affect the world of the play and the other characters in ways they do and do not know. This is particularly clear because Shakespeare's secondary characters are so complex. His plots can also start in medias res. And despite the dramatic resolutions which most often include death, they would almost always have a stimulating sequel, while some go as far as demanding sequels (these might exist, like with the Henriad, or not, like with Love's Labour's Lost). Shakespeare does this to some extent in The Merry Wives of Windsor, re-presenting the popular Falstaff from the Henry IV plays. How fascinating would a play be if it were centred on Lady Macbeth or Claudius or even Juliet's nurse? And a sequel about whether things work out for Benedick and Beatrice in *Much Ado About Nothing*, or how Fortinbras copes with the foreseeable civil unrest that follows such a tumultuous period in Elsinore's history? Terror shows how death is not a resolution: after the death of the suicide bomber or the execution of a plotter or even the passing away of a victim, the impact still reverberates.

Taking these ideas into account, perhaps the responses to Shakespeare, positive and negative, stem from the very vitality of the plays, plots, and characters. Discussing this vitality with Fernie, he explained:

> Morally and ethically and politically we need to take account of it. And when we're worrying through problems of evil and terror and so forth, it's important that we recognise the appeal, the excitement of those sorts of stories and their enactment, and that we're morally honest about it. So for my money, there is a kind of dangerous vitality in Shakespeare, but part of the task of morality and culture and social welfare is to accommodate for the real facts of human moral life.[6]

These facts might include the polarised state of society. We should hardly be surprised about the obvious corollary, that one state's perceived terrorist is another state's freedom fighter. And this can become even more apparent in Shakespeare's plays. He even alludes to the human propensity for dichotomy, for example, in *Love's Labour's Lost*, where despite all the ups and downs, the final lines of the play (added in the Folio) make binary separation blatantly clear (even the lines are split):

You that way;

we this way.
(5.2.927–28)

To add to that, the potential for polarised opinions is boundless. First, due to the complexity of Shakespeare's characters, and second, due to the potential for and history of mutually contradictory interpretations and appropriations of his works. So on one end of the spectrum, Shakespeare could be interpreted as a symbol of Western supremacy; but on another, his works are steeped in terroristic actions and justifications, even role models. Not only did he know terrorism at close hand, he appears to have used that understanding to create some of his multidimensional figures. Not monsters, but human beings. In doing so and through an *intentional vitality* – a vitality that is both intentional on his part and vitalises the consideration of intentionalism – Shakespeare does not necessarily justify or condemn or even explain. He explores.

ARS LONGA, VITA BREVIS

In 1822, on a stage in Baltimore, Maryland, Othello is about to smother Desdemona to death. At that moment, a US soldier sitting in the audience pulls out his firearm and shoots the lead actor before breaking his arm. Stendhal reports that the soldier shouted as he did so: "It will never be said that in my presence a damn negro kills a white woman".[7] The problems raised by this incident are numerous: the racism cannot go unmentioned and neither can this soldier's skewed perception of his duty. Over the centuries, there have been many such incidents during Othello in particular, no doubt fuelled by sympathy for the white woman and indignation at the black man. Women have screamed to warn Desdemona and men have bawled to threaten Othello or Iago. Shakespeare's vitality means we should come to expect viewpoints, interpretations, and absolute decisions to be conjuring, stirring, and materialising both on the stage and off it – often in the moment. These coincide with audience members' innermost thoughts, fears, and prejudices. But they are also informed by the society and context around them. In this case, and even through today, it's a society in which there is an ongoing discomfort with relationships across racial lines, with white women's tears, and with black masculinity (note the link with the War on Terror's narrative about saving women from the men of colour's oppression). If Shakespeare can help elucidate aspects of identity, whether individual or collective, then it is also natural that those searching for and justifying their identity might find solace in liking or disliking him.[8]

There exists a fine and faint line between reality and fiction, between life and art. But fictional art can and does push humans to the limits of their emotions. And yet, we are expected to comprehend the fictional nature and artistic creativity and metatheatrical tropes – and therefore not react outwardly. Is that actually fair? Where should we be releasing these building energies? We see this today with the digital world, as YouTube algorithms take us down a rabbit hole from one video to the next. These video suggestions create echo chambers in which one ends up seeing only one side of the story. Their content also begins more moderately and turns more extreme over time. Yet we become surprised when the culture we feed off results in action or imitation – like when an Internet addict goes on a chauvinistic shooting spree or conspiracy theorists storm the Capitol Building. When life imitates algorithm. Somehow, and in line with broken pseudo-democratic political systems (where two-party systems and safe electoral seats reign) in addition to enforced, blind consumerism, the expectation is to be a passive consumer of art despite its raging emotions and proven ability to rage our own emotions. So where is the closure for an audience member or reader? How can the audience member or reader actually vocalise their reception of the art? (Can chatting to friends or attending the post-show director's talk really be enough?) The creation of a mainstream leads to the creation of an opposition. Silence leads to release. And being forcefully silenced can lead to extreme reaction.

Furthermore, the spill into reality is a reminder of how art is ineffably dynamic. It changes based on the many social, political, and cultural contexts around it and in turn affects those contexts. These contexts affect and are affected by reception, the single most powerful way a practically unchanging text can indeed change. And as noted, I believe that Shakespeare's plays can be differentiated as texts and works. The texts are the words and the works remove the text from its isolation to consider it alongside everything that comes with it, including the contexts and afterlives.

When it comes to terror, there is an inextricable relationship between it on one hand and aesthetic emotion on another. But there remains a general anger when something seemingly unreal spills into reality. And yet we still watch. Issues surrounding murder, rape, and consent have long formed creative plots but in an ideal world, should remain unimaginable in our own lives. Pornography remains so popular that a staggering one-third of all downloads on the Internet are pornographic – and this appears to be tolerable as long as what happens on the screen stays on the screen. And violent videos about terror and beheadings by ISIS are watched by millions (it seems fine to do so if it's on a documentary, rather than via extremist outlets). When it comes to Shakespeare's plots, we have one unacceptable deed after another. The gore (think of the executions, dismemberment, and cannibalism of *Titus Andronicus* or the eye-gouging and back-stabbing of *King Lear*), the sexual violence and personal violation (*The Rape of Lucrece*), the disregard for sexual consent (*Measure for Measure*), the physical and emotional domestic abuse (*The Taming of the Shrew*), the violent, forceful usurpation (*Richard III*), and so on. If these works represent an imagined world that we do not want to emulate or spill into reality, then where and how can society draw that line between art and life? When an extremist reacts to Shakespeare, the play has already arrived into the real world and there is nothing we can do about it.

The normalised topography of fear and violence is present in and through Shakespeare's canon simply because it has always existed, albeit in different ways. Today, it takes a different and more available form through digital access, as one millennial's viral tweet jested: "I loved growing up with the internet in the early 2000s! I played flash games, I took care of neopets, I saw a beheading video when I was 12, I made friends on myspace". And given the content of Shakespeare's works, one could even argue that Shakespeare requires a warning disclaimer. This has in fact been done recently. For example, in 2013, the Shakespeare Theatre Company's *Measure for Measure* placed a red-lettered "18+" warning on its website.[9] In 2017, student timetables at Cambridge University included "trigger warnings" in the form of "red triangles with an exclamation mark" next to the week on *The Comedy of Errors* and *Titus Andronicus*.[10]

But audiences flocked to Shakespeare's violent plays. Until the eighteenth century in England, seeing an execution was something of a family outing. And if viewer ratings are anything to go by these days, much of the world's population is attracted to violent spectacle. But why do humans gravitate to watching violence? The spiritual teacher Eckhart Tolle notes how we indulge in a barrage of negative news and violent shows to the extent that species from another planet would be amazed "that millions of people love and pay money to watch humans kill and inflict pain on each other and call it 'entertainment'". Tolle theorises how humans carry a "pain-body" that feeds on emotional unhappiness and suffering, which "in addition to reactivity, negative thinking, and personal drama … renews itself vicariously through" the violence we view.[11] Or perhaps by observing violence we are making contact with repressed ideas: an attempt, to use Carl Jung's terms, to "integrate" our "shadows" (unconscious parts of ourselves that we don't identify with, but that might be capable of atrocity). It makes sense, then, that Prophet Muhammad defined the "greater jihad" (literally meaning struggle) as nothing to do with an enemy or war, but "jihad against oneself". So is there something about witnessing the birth of a monster that appeals and maybe even heals? For Jung, at least, embodying our "shadows" can stop them from getting denser and darker. Indeed, through the activity of reception, we are active players in the violence, so much so that we have become desensitised to death statistics and gory images.

Literature and the arts come into this as a type of release – essentially a type of freedom – in which we can observe, embody, and enjoy things that we would ordinarily frown upon. Theatre, then, is a purposeful non-truth. The potential problem here, though, is that overusing "the world's a stage" (*As You Like* 2.7.142) notion of theatre as a metaphor for life can also become, first, an underestimation of the impact of art, and second, an underestimation of the impact of real events. Yes, art imitates life and life imitates art. It is a cyclical, infinite process. Shakespeare portrays terror in his art because in life humans have always been perpetrators or victims of varying terrors: "The fault, dear Brutus, is not in our stars / But in ourselves" (*Julius Caesar* 1.2.146–47). It is also predominantly life – in the form of the context and reception around the creative work – that changes, thus complicating the interpretative process so that neither art nor life can remain static and so that the cycle can continue in perpetuity. As Hippocrates summarised two and a half millennia ago, "Life is short, art is long … judgement is difficult". And as Nietzsche notes, "We have art in order not to die of the truth".

In the case of Shakespeare and terrorism, it is through a prism of absolute decisions, of contemplating our route towards achieving morality or identity, that we can at least reinterpret Hamlet's state of mind and contemplation as a cry for freedom – and his failure to achieve this through peaceful means leads him on a path towards violence. On one hand, the characters created by Shakespeare, and the way extremists have responded to the figure and works, whether with despisal or with admiration, help explain and confirm aspects of the terrorist mindset as well as the paradigms and frameworks that generate and combat terrorism and its narratives. On another hand, clichés aside, to my mind, I'm now more sure than ever that Shakespeare does explore the human condition. Our constant search for identity, our desire for freedom, our longing for expression: all of these are paramount to his plots and themes, to the contexts of his own life, and to our continued receptions of his works. But our means of reaching these differ vastly, and on the extreme end of the scale, have led to terror.

NOTES

1   This discussion of first impressions is adapted from my BBC Radio 3 column: Islam Issa, "Who Ever Loved that Loved Not at First Sight", *BBC Radio 3* (12 June 2017), www.bbc.co.uk/programmes/p055bg9w. I am grateful to Ewan Fernie for alerting me to Miranda's first impressions. Also note that her name originates from the Latin verb "to wonder", and, in turn, when Ferdinand sees her, his reaction is "O, you wonder!" (1.2.494). The note on *Macbeth* appeared in my exhibition *Shakespeare in South Asia* at the Shakespeare Birthplace Trust (2017–18).

2   Hans Robert Jauss, *Toward an Aesthetic of Reception*, trans. Timothy Bahti (Brighton: Harvester, 1982), 185. It is worth noting Jauss has recently and concerningly been linked with the terrorising Nazi regime, which can complicate (and render ironic) this striking theoretical statement.

3   *The Simpsons* satirised the lack of nuance and inexperience of "social justice warriors" and how the figure and works of Shakespeare can easily find their way into social justice conversations when the show portrayed Yale University students holding up a "SHAKESPEARE IS MURDER" banner to the dismay of wealthy conservative Mr. Burns – "The Caper Chase", dir. Lance Kramer, *The Simpsons* season 28, episode 19 (2017).

4   On *periphery neglect*, see Issa, *Milton in the Arab-Muslim World*; Islam Issa, "How Literature Shapes History", in *What Is History, Now*, ed. Helen Carr and Suzannah Lipscomb (London: Weidenfeld & Nicholson, 2021). Both of these sources also indicate ways in which *periphery neglect* can help predict political events. On the *entry point*, see Issa, "How Literature Shapes History".

5   In the case of spectacular violence, it has been argued that earlier in his career, this was predominantly to entertain, while the later plays consider how humans engage in gratuitous violence. See R. A. Foakes, *Shakespeare and Violence* (Cambridge: Cambridge University Press, 2003).

6   Fernie, in Issa, "Shakespeare and Terrorism", unpublished recording.

7   Stendhal, *Racine et Shakespeare*, ed. L. Vincent (Paris: Librairie Hatier, 1927), 10. Translation from French is my own. It is unclear from Stendhal's account whether the actor was black or in "blackface".

8   For instance, superficial utilisation of Shakespeare quotations or portraits on social media presents an aspect of this. Quotations have

been used to boast of sophistication and wellness on one hand, or to incite violent opinion on another. For instance, a Yemeni Twitter account supporting the armed Houthi movement displays a cartoon of Shakespeare holding a machine gun as its profile picture.

9 Nelson Pressley, "Warning! Shakespeare for 18 and Above", *Washington Post* (20 September 2013), www.washingtonpost.com/entertainment/theater_dance/warning-shakespeare-for-18-and-above/2013/09/19/5697dc74-1f99-11e3-9ad0-96244100e647_story.html [accessed 10 September 2019].

10 "Cambridge Uni Students Get Shakespeare Trigger Warnings", *BBC News* (19 October 2017), www.bbc.co.uk/news/uk-england-cambridgeshire-41678937 [accessed 10 September 2019].

11 Eckhart Tolle, *A New Earth: Create a Better Life* (London: Penguin, 2016), 152–53.

Index